Heidelberg
Science
Library

Philip Kraft

Programmers
and Managers

The Routinization of
Computer Programming
in the United States

Springer-Verlag
New York
Heidelberg
Berlin

Philip Kraft
Department of Sociology
State University of New York
    at Binghamton
Binghamton, New York 13901

Library of Congress Cataloging in Publication Data

Kraft, Philip.
    Programmers and managers.

    (Heidelberg science library)
    Bibliography: p.
    Includes index.
    1. Computer programmers—United States.   2. Elec-
tronic data processing departments—Personnel management.
3. Industrial relations.   I. Title.   II. Series.
HD8039.D37K7   331.7′61′0016420973   77-1667

Printed in the United States of America.

9 8 7 6 5 4 3 2 1

ISBN 0-387-90248-1   Springer-Verlag   New York

ISBN 3-540-90248-1   Springer-Verlag   Berlin   Heidelberg

Foreword

Norbert Wiener, perhaps better than anyone else, understood the intimate and delicate relationship between control and communication: that messages intended as commands do not necessarily differ from those intended simply as facts. Wiener noted the paradox when the modern computer was hardly more than a laboratory curiosity. Thirty years later, the same paradox is at the heart of a severe identity crisis which confronts computer programmers. Are they primarily members of "management" acting as foremen, whose task it is to ensure that orders emanating from executive suites are faithfully translated into comprehensible messages? Or are they perhaps simply engineers preoccupied with the technical difficulties of relating "software" to "hardware" and vice versa? Are they aware, furthermore, of the degree to which their work—whether as manager or engineer—routinizes the work of others and thereby helps shape the structure of social class relationships?

I doubt that many of us who lived through the first heady and frantic years of software development—at places like the RAND and System Development Corporations—ever took time to think about such questions. The science fiction-like setting of mysterious machines, blinking lights, and torrents of numbers served to awe outsiders who could only marvel at the complexity of it all. We were insiders who constituted a secret society into which only initiates were welcome.

So today I marvel at the boundless audacity of a rank outsider in writing a book like *Programmers and Managers*.

What can be said of this study?

To begin with Dr. Kraft has written a study of computer

programmers unlike any other study of computer programmers. I am simply overwhelmed at what he has managed to learn about the profession, the workplace, and the spirit of computer programming. To my knowledge, this is the first study written from the perspective of programmers themselves. There is, of course, an enormous literature in this area, characteristically written from the perspective of either the hardware (essentially an engineering perspective) or the process to be automated (essentially a management perspective). When Dr. Kraft observes that the limited material available about programmers is not concerned with trying to understand who and what programmers are but rather with developing techniques to control them, he is being accurate in a way which only a genuine "insider" can appreciate. I suspect that countless programmers, reading his account, will indeed experience "the shock of recognizing something which had always been there but hadn't been thought about before."

But this is more than a study of computer programmers written for members of the profession. In providing a clearly stated brief history of the modern computer in terms which all laypeople can readily comprehend, Dr. Kraft has provided an important demystification service in a field which thrives on obfuscation and inflated technical pretense. He has, in addition, provided important insights into the bureaucratic environment within which nearly all programmers must work. Even more significantly, he has also provided insights into the relationships between routinization of work in contemporary industrial society and developing social class relationships.

I suspect this work will be somewhat controversial for many years to come. In the first place, it is clearly not a routine piece of work done in a conventional manner. Since it is not, many professionals in both computer science and sociology may experience considerable difficulty in relating to it. Sociologists who can understand the broader social implications of the phenomena being discussed characteristically know very little about the technology or the minutae of the environment in which computer programmers work. And those who are familiar with the environment either do not know or do not wish to be told about some of the social realities involved.

Dr. Kraft has in a remarkable way fashioned a book which fills the gaps in both fields.

May 1977

Robert Boguslaw
Department of Sociology
Washington University
St. Louis, Missouri

Acknowledgments

Because *Programmers and Managers* itself must be considered a preface to more and better conceived studies of technical occupations and technical workers, I will limit myself here to thanking those who offered help, criticism, and guidance. The people who provided the best of these—programmers, managers, systems analysts, and others who make their living in the software industry—cannot be acknowledged by name. More's the pity, since the debt is all the greater.

Fortunately, I am able to thank directly many people who insisted on being useful, sometimes in spite of doubts or reservations about what I was doing. They are, by accident of alphabetical priority, Cathy Arnst, Robert Boguslaw, Laird Cummings, Pat Dolaway, Daniel Freedman, James Geschwender, Joan Greenbaum, David Gries, Nancy Hall, Mel Leiman, David Noble, James O'Connor, Barry Truchil, and Nancy Zimmet.

The American Sociological Association, through its Committee on Problems of the Discipline, was nice enough to give money to several sociologists to explore issues raised by the study of white collar workers. My colleagues in that undertaking—Theodore Kaplan, John Low-Beer, Martin Oppenheimer, Theodore Reed and Magali Sarfatti-Larson—asked and answered questions, provided reassurance in times of doubt, injected doubts at times of over-assurance, and generally acted like colleagues are supposed to act. I am most grateful to them and to the ASA for allowing us to get together.

The Research Foundation of the State University of New York funded a small preliminary study of programmers through its faculty grants program. Their early support is gratefully acknowledged.

Philip Kraft

Binghamton, New York
January 1977

Contents

4 The programmer's workplace: Part I the "shop"   64

5 The programmer's workplace: Part II careers, pay, and professionalism   80

6 The routinization of computer programming   97

Introduction

Programmers, managers, and sociologists

Introductions traditionally are places where authors make one last heroic attempt to justify their work—and to cover their tracks. It is, all things considered, a useful tradition and I too would like to explain how and why this study of computer programmers came to be written.

I live and work near Binghamton, New York. Because IBM is here, because General Electric, Singer-Link, GAF, and dozens of more modest enterprises are here, lots of computer programmers are here too. In the normal course of things, I got to know many of them as neighbors, students, and colleagues. From the start they struck me as marginal people. They did not, for example, fit neatly into the stereotypes that are commonly applied, however unjustly, to engineering workers as a whole. They did not look like engineers are supposed to look (crew-cuts, narrow ties, penny loafers, etc.), nor were they taciturn and awkward around nonprogrammers. They did not appear to be particularly conservative, either politically or socially. Many were women.

But if programmers could "pass" as nonengineers in a nonengineering world, they were not exactly academics or managers or salespeople either. In a word, they were different in ways I couldn't quite define and I got curious. Since my major interests are in the area of work and occupations, a study of computer specialists seemed a natural way of satisfying my curiosity in an orderly and systematic manner.

So I began, in an orderly and systematic manner, to collect information about programmers. I wanted to learn about their history and the history of their field, their education, their occupational backgrounds, distribution, and so on. Almost immediately I encountered one major problem: hardly any information about these things existed. What little material did exist was of a very peculiar sort. It was obviously intended for managers and personnel directors rather than for the world in general. I don't mean to suggest that there was some sort of deliberate conspiracy involved. It seemed instead to be a peculiar case of an exotic occupation whose obscurity was penetrated only by those in whose interest it was to do so, i.e., managers.

This made me all the more curious, particularly since computer programmers are critical people whose role in data processing is, to put it charitably, little appreciated. It was easy enough to understand why sociologists and other social scientists had, in effect, abandoned programmers to their obscurity. Computers are still relatively new and largely mysterious. Social scientists, even those who make regular use of the hardware, too often are only dimly aware that the machines which do the things they have come to take for granted have to be told what to do by people. Furthermore, it saddens me to say, sociologists cling with most of the rest of the population to a stereotype of engineering and technical workers which extends to computer specialists as well. Engineers, goes the old saw, are dull people. If they don't actually wear brush-cuts and white socks anymore, they remain social Neanderthals. They are "thing-oriented" rather than "people-oriented." They have no interests other than their work, which is, in any case, so esoteric as to be meaningless even to the specialists who do it. And what is perhaps the unkindest cut of all, technical workers are hypocritical political cretins who affect a philosophy of rugged individualism even as they earn a major portion of their incomes from government contracts. They are, in short, nowhere as interesting (or romantic) as the autoworkers or the physicians or streetwalkers that social scientists usually have preferred to study.

By contrast, management researchers have shown considerably more interest. They have compiled an extensive—if, for all intents and purposes, also an underground—literature on computer programmers and other computer workers. More accurately, they have compiled four distinct literatures. The first is a version of the old Norman Vincent Peale/Dale Carnegie brand of moral uplift. Managers are encouraged to develop proper attitudes towards themselves and the programmers who work under them. Their duty is to foster right-thinking, enthusiasm for the job, and loyalty to the company. This is the sort of stuff that gets recited at management conventions and then reprinted in house journals as inspirational material for up and coming junior executives. Except for its anthropological interest to students of managerial mythology, most of it can be safely ignored.

The second kind has to do with what is usually called psychological profiling. Employers commonly make use of tests which they hope will provide them with clues to the psychological makeup of potential employees. The tests themselves have a number of purposes. One is to predict how well an individual is likely to perform certain kinds of job-related tasks. Programmer aptitude tests are perhaps the best-known examples. Others are concerned with fingering potential "troublemakers," that is, anyone who might disagree with his or her betters or is not likely to adopt pro-company attitudes. In spite of their long history of use by industry, there is considerable disagreement about their accuracy and usefulness and much management literature has been concerned with these tests' relative merits.

A third kind of management writing is of more immediate interest. It consists of the information about programmers' salaries, their distribution by job categories, by industry, and so on. To the extent that this sort of information is accurate it is, of course, very useful. Unfortunately, there is relatively little of it—*Datamation* and *Infosystems* seem to be carrying most of the burden alone—and it applies to something less than the whole population of programmers.

The fourth and last major category is made up of the work of highly experienced programmers who have spent considerable time analyzing the organization of the programming workplace. These writings are fascinating for more than their technical content; the work of F. T. Baker, Harlan Mills, and Gerald M. Weinberg, for example, is also important *politically*. This is a critical and often misunderstood point. The social relations of the workplace are arrangements of people which affect more than just efficiency and productivity. They are also relations of power, of domination and subordination. In the workplace, including the programming workplace, such relations are most clearly expressed in the form of a hierarchy (sometimes referred to as the "chain of command" or "career ladder") and usually represented by formal organizational charts. Mills, Baker, and Weinberg, to the extent they and others like them explore the social relations between various categories of programmers, between programmers and their managers, among programming departments, between programming departments and other departments in the organization, are all discussing questions having to do with who is in charge of whom and what. They are, in other words, discussing profoundly political relationships.

Because most managers understand this, the most serious and thoughtful work of management researchers (and their academic counterparts in Schools of Management) focuses on issues which are not technical in nature; they are concerned primarily instead with ways of arranging people to make them amenable to management influence. Discussions of such varied concerns as "dual ladders" (career lines for technical employees), "structured programming," "chief programmer teams," and "egoless" programming (all ways of arranging programmers in particular forms of hierarchy), job structuring, and so on, whatever their technical content, are *primarily discussions of how to manage, not necessarily of how to increase efficiency.*

Put another way, management literature on programmers displays a general concern with developing techniques to get the people managers manage to do what they are told, not simply how to write better programs. It tends to concentrate on ways of figuring out how to predict who can do what kinds of programming jobs ("personnel selection"), how to get programmers to fit into the structure of the organization ("getting on board" or, occasionally, "seeing the Big Picture"), and, all things being equal, to get as much work out of them as possible ("developing motivation" and "acquiring the right attitude").

Finally, it must also be said that much of this management literature is not very flattering to programmers. Some of it, in fact, closely resembles the popular stereotypes of engineering and other technical workers. The major difference is that while such stereotypes have been used to justify social sneers or to ignore programmers altogether, managers have used similar stereotypes to create techniques to advance their own very specific ends. Managers, for example, are quite happy to go along with the popularly held notion that programmers are "thing-oriented" rather than "people-oriented." A common managerial position is that, left to themselves, programmers "would design a system for the computer not for the user." There are endless variations on this theme alone.

What all of this added up to, it seemed to me, was that the limited material about programmers was not concerned with trying to understand who and what programmers were; it was concerned instead with developing techniques to control them. Although managerial wisdom with respect to programmers constituted the bulk of the available material about them, clearly I was also going to have to look elsewhere for less self-serving information.

Expanding the data base

Partly to balance the obvious managerial orientation of most writings on programmers and partly to gather information that was not readily available, I undertook a series of interviews with many different kinds of programmers—systems programmers, applications programmers, programmers who worked for hardware companies, for software companies, for universities, for hospitals, and for commercial and industrial organizations. I also managed to talk with a very rare species, the middle-aged-to-old programmer, and I also came across a hitherto undiscovered one: the unemployed programmer. For good measure, I talked with managers and with people generally referred to as systems analysts. I also talked with academic people who are training (or trying to figure out how to train) programmers in universities. Finally, where I could, I observed programmers at work.

Whenever I reached some sort of conclusion, I wrote it up and showed it to several of the programmers I had talked with earlier for their comment and criticism. I did this for several reasons. The most obvious was that I wanted to be sure of the facts of a situation and to catch any glaring errors in reporting what I had seen or heard. A second reason was largely a matter of principle. I have never admired the ethics or methodology of social scientists who act as "participant observers" and insert themselves into a community to report on the "natives." I don't approve because the temptation is almost always too great to resist treating the "natives" as objects. If people are good enough to let you bother them with questions and constant hovering around, they have a right to learn what you've learned and to know what you think of them.

But beyond issues of accuracy and principle, returning to the people I had interviewed or observed produced some unanticipated results. For one thing, many programmers who had been the most thoughtful and the most helpful to me hadn't realized just how clearly they had analyzed their own work experiences and personal histories. They had put together, a piece at a time and scattered over one or two interview sessions, a cogent picture of what it was like to be a programmer. When I returned to them with a "story" constructed from their own observations, there was invariably the shock of recognizing something which had always been there but hadn't been thought about before. Recognition prompted more thought, more details, and new insight.

This was obviously a fruitful method for probing beneath

the top layer of programmers' existence. It was also personally gratifying because the programmers themselves played an active, rather than a passive, role in that probing, something which made the entire undertaking more legitimate for me, as well as making it more productive. But after several such experiences something struck me with particular force. Most programmers seemed to know well enough how their jobs were organized, at least insofar as knowing means they possessed most of the information. On the other hand, few seemed to understand what they knew. They had little in the way of an overall perspective which could tie together all the miscellaneous bits of information they all possessed. Everyone was conscious of career developments, of relations with managers, and so on, but these very structured, very carefully defined relations which made up their workplaces were typically looked upon as individual, rather than organizational, relations. Relationships, for example, between a programmer and a manager were almost always viewed as personal ones, rather than as part of an overall structure which individuals were inserted into or removed from as the requirements of the organization demanded.

It would not be correct to say, however, that programmers as a group had no overall perspective of any kind. They did and, not surprisingly, it closely resembled what their managers told them was the case. I was astounded by how routinely and without much objection programmers accepted their managers' point of view, although it came nowhere close to accurately describing the programmers' real situation. If, for example, programmers were part of a large work force conceived of and treated by higher management as an undifferentiated aggregate, even those who worked in such environments remained convinced that their own positions were determined almost exclusively by their individual performance and their private relationship with their particular managers. I encountered, for example, a nearly total lack of accurate information about how salaries were arrived at (a touchy subject, discussed more fully in Chapter 5). Similar misinformation characterized their understanding of how the promotional structure operated, of how older (i.e., 35-year-old) programmers were regularly "recycled" out of programming, and even of the job categories which made up the data processing staff.

Obviously, this raised a whole new set of questions for me to deal with. *Why* were these intelligent, thoughtful people so relatively uninformed about how the organizations which employed them actually operated? Why were they so predisposed to accept their managers' version of how things operated; versions which, to an outsider at least, clearly did not correspond to what seemed to be really going on? Did the semi-secretive nature of most management literature on programmers have any connection with either the programmers' relative ignorance of their own situation or with their willingness to accept whatever they had been told?

More interviewing answered some of these questions—and raised some new ones. The interviews of managers in particular made me aware of just how much like other work programming was being organized and structured. In personal interviews as much as in published statements, managers made it clear that they were not willing to leave the on the job behavior of their programmers to either luck or goodwill or even to constant barrages of company propaganda. They were taking great pains to formalize and regularize workplace structure and organization in order to assure themselves control over the people they managed. The development of "job standards," the emergence of increasingly specialized job descriptions, the obvious efforts to reduce overall job skill levels through extensive use of canned programs, structured programming, and hardware innovation—all of these things were, to a social scientist, straightforward efforts to make the social relations of programming like, say, those of the machine shop or the secretarial pool or the drafting room.

Programmers, for the most part, seemed unaware of this process and generally believed that they occupied special, unique positions and enjoyed the personal protection of their managers. A system of routinization and standardization was being developed and implemented, yet programmers still held to the belief that their roles in computing organization would go on as they had in the past.

Was there anything about the structure of the programmers' workplace that could explain this? What techniques of workplace management encouraged programmers to accept their employers' view of the "Big Picture?" Conversely, were there any aspects of their workplace that encouraged programmers to resist or reinterpret what their managers wanted them to believe? Was there perhaps anything in their educational experiences which made management's efforts easier or harder? And finally, was there anything in the nature of the programmers' work itself which either managers or programmers have seized on in structuring their on the job social relations with each other?

I have not approached these questions in a completely disinterested way. In trying to make sense of the information gathered through interviews, observing programmers at work, talking with their managers, attending management "seminars" and industry conventions, and, generally, hanging around a lot of programmers, it was apparent that managers and their employers knew something that programmers didn't know. It was also apparent that because of this managers were also in a position to exert a degree of influence over programmers that was not—and could not be—balanced in any meaningful way. It seemed to me, in other words, that programmers and other computer people were at a distinct disadvantage in their dealings with their managers in the matter of how their day to day existence in the workplace was to be organized.

Quite frankly, I have become a partisan on the side of programmers. If, however, I have not remained disinterested, I have tried, nonetheless, to be as objective as I can. This is, I know, a hard position to accept for those who are convinced that objectivity equals noninvolvement, even in the social sciences. The debate is an old one which has not yet been settled to anyone's satisfaction. Whether it is settled satisfactorily here, I can only suggest that the reader, after evaluating this particular study, make up her or his own mind.

How this study is organized

In *Programmers and Managers* I have proceeded from a description of what programmers do to an analysis of how managers organize programmers to do it. For the sake of nonprogrammers, I have included a brief history of the modern computer and an even briefer history of the development of programming languages. For the sake of programmers, I have spent some time discussing the nature of bureaucracy and hierarchy, primarily because so much of the programmer's workplace experience takes place in and is shaped by bureaucratic organization. The chapter by chapter sequence is as follows. Chapter 1 examines the tools of the programmer's trade, by and for whom they were developed, as well as the efforts of managers to simplify the programmer's work in order to integrate it into conventional industrial organizations. Chapter 2 continues the discussion of simplification and standardization by focusing on the varieties of programmer training now available, where training is offered, and to what kinds of people. Chapter 3 analyzes in detail some of the major technical-social innovations introduced by the computer industry as part of its continuing efforts to reduce the skills of most programmers. Chapter 4 looks at the physical arrangement of the "typical" programmer workplace to see how management-introduced changes in the way programming is done have found expression in the way the programming workplace is organized. Chapter 5 extends the analysis of the programmer workplace to the areas of pay, careers, and ideology; emphasis here is on the use of salary increments, promotions, and an ideology of "professionalism" to encourage programmer individualism—if not individuality—and discourage collective organization, notably unions. Chapter 6 is the required exercise in inspiration and prediction, although I have made every effort not to overdo it.

A note on software scientists

I have called this study *Programmers and Managers* rather than *Programmers, Managers, and Scientists* because it says relatively little about the men and women who have produced the great hardware and software advances of the past two decades. If they have received short shrift it has not been for a lack of appreciation of their role but because I have wanted to stress how managers have applied technical advances to the organization of the electronic data processing workplace.

This has made it necessary to examine what managers have selected from the work of edp researchers in order to further their own ends, ends which are invariably informed by the desire to reduce costs and increase profits. Researchers usually have other—or at least additional—priorities: solving a problem, making something work, or simply understanding something that they do not understand now. Their discoveries and inventions are not necessarily useful to managers unless carefully modified to meet the latter's own, very particular needs.

Structured programming is perhaps the most striking example of this managerial selection process. In *Programmers and Managers* I have described structured programming as many managers and programmers see it; I have suggested that managers use structured programming to de-skill and control their programmers. Yet, there is nothing inherent in the principles of structured programming—at least as put forward by people like Edsger Dijkstra, David Gries, and many others—which suggests that its developers are concerned with anything except making the writing of programs a more clear-headed and self-conscious undertaking than it presently is. (See also Chapter 3, footnote 5). Indeed, Dijkstra and Gries have stressed in their writings that they see in structured programming the possibility of enlarging, rather than diminishing, the skills, knowledge, and understanding of the average programmer. I have no doubt whatsoever that they believe and hope this to be the case.

Unfortunately, this is not the issue. Whatever the intentions of software scientists, it will be edp managers, not scientists, who decide the manner in which scientific innovations will be applied to the problems of profit-making and employee control. We are, of course, confronting here a specific example of the much broader question of the relation between science, engineering, and the organization of the economic system. While a fundamental issue, the broader question has not been addressed here, in part because I have focused on a much narrower problem and in part because others, notably David Noble in his path-breaking *America by Design,* have already grappled with it much better than I could hope to.

I hope, in short, that computer scientists will not take my analysis of how managers manage as an implied criticism of their own motives.

1 Computers and the people who make them work

Most people now alive were born after the development of the modern computer. We are by now used to the fact that our electric bills, bank statements, and income tax returns are processed by high-speed machines for whom we represent a pattern of electric charges and nothing else. We are also aware, if somewhat more dimly, that the subway we take to work or school, the traffic lights that regulate our daily commute, and the elevators that take us up and down skyscrapers are likely to be controlled by automatic machines instead of people. We tend to be even less aware of how, with the help of computers, our workplaces have been taken apart and reassembled to change the way we make things. Yet, these are only the most visible changes wrought by the widespread application of computer-based technology. Automated subways and computer-controlled production lines are hard to miss if we happen to deal with them every day. The consequences of econometric modeling and computerized war-games are harder to see and even harder to properly appreciate. Increasingly as a matter of routine, however, goods and services are produced only after elaborate calculations are made about demand, cost, resources, and profitability. These are not, let me stress, the abstract, idle figurings of economists or technicians. What products we buy and therefore what jobs we will have, whether there will be tight money or inflation or both, whether the government will send troops to some distant corner of the globe, are decisions some people have made or will make on the basis of information processed for them by computers. The computer, in other words, can no longer be considered a curious, if complicated, toy of interest only to specialists or science-fiction enthusiasts. It has become so much of a commonplace that the lack of popular understanding of its impact underscores just how much a part of our everyday lives the computer has become.

There is, however, still an aura of magic surrounding computers and electronic data processing—"edp"—in general. But little magic is involved. In spite of fanciful talk about artificial intelligence and all those bad movies starring talking computers, the machine itself can only sit there, quite still and quite useless, until someone—a real, live human being—plugs it in and then supplies it with detailed operating instructions. Broadly speaking, the instructions are of two kinds. The first signal the machine to process a specific set of numerical information in a desired way and then either display the results or use them to control the operation of a connected device. These are more and more being provided by nonspecialists. A bank clerk who enters my account number on a keyboard (technically, a "remote-entry terminal" connected to a central computer) and then punches a few more keys will get a display of my current balance. Similarly, anyone who directly dials a long-distance call instructs a computer to locate a particular telephone, activate its signal, make the connection, calculate the cost, and charge it to the appropriate account.

Before any of these things can be done, however, the machine has to be given another and much more elaborate set of instructions in order to operate properly—or at all for that matter. Again, the reason has little to do with magic. Computers are machines made up of circuits which alter electric current and are altered by it. Machines, of course, can't decide which of their circuits will be used to carry out a given operation, nor can they decide which operations to perform in the first place. Computing machines, let it be said at the outset and as clearly as possible, can't decide *anything*. Someone has to decide—ahead of time—what the machine will do and how it will do it. People have to "prime" the machine, in other words, so that once appropriate instructions have been entered and the proper buttons have been pushed, the computer can go through the correct sequence of operations.[1]

Obviously, then, every computer operation requires a great

---

[1]Some admirers of the computer's decision-making abilities may take offense at my assessment of the limits of artificial intelligence. It is true that the machines can do wonderful things, but it is important to understand what exactly they are doing. Primarily, they do what they are told to do. Machines

deal of painstaking human preparation and obviously such preparation is considerably more complex and time-consuming than, for example, dialing a telephone number. But here is a major paradox: the simpler the final instructions given a computer—those typed in by a bank teller, or by a billings clerk—the more elaborate the preparatory work, the "wiring in" of the smallest details of every machine operation. It takes only a few seconds for a bank clerk to retrieve my account balance, but it takes months, perhaps longer, for specialists to design, write, test, correct, and finally install the software[2] before the computer can be used. Once installed, quantities can be manipulated at speeds calculated in nanoseconds. When there are large amounts of information to be processed in roughly similar ways, the extensive preparation is more than worth the effort, time, and money it requires.

The paradox—the need for complex preparation in order to make the machines simple to use—simultaneously divides and unites everyone connected with computers. It will reappear in various forms throughout this study, but for now it serves to underline the basic, if also the most widely misunderstood, characteristic of modern computers: if we live in a society organized around magic "black boxes," those boxes, in the last analysis, do nothing unless told to by human beings. The computer may have entered every nook and cranny of our lives, but it has been taken there one tiny step at a time by people. The "magic" of computers and edp is no more and no less than human imagination and skill.

The division of labor in programming

The people who take computers wherever they go are called, of course, computer programmers. The title, like so much

---

can make decisions about what chess or checker piece to move, which machines to turn off or on, and so on, but all such decisions (or the guidelines according to which the decisions are made) have to be anticipated by people who program the machine. These anticipatory decisions and guidelines—not to say the original decision to play checkers or regulate an assembly line—are made by people, not by machines with even the most elaborate "decision-making" capabilities. The issue here is *intent,* not logic.

[2]"Software" is the general term, now standard in the computer industry, for the instructions which control the computer's operation. Such instructions are thus distinguished from the machines themselves which are called, logically enough, "hardware."

However, one of the important developments of the last decade has been to blur the distinction as computers have had more and more of their instructions permanently entered or "wired in." See pp. 27–29.

In this study, the terms software worker and programmer are used more or less interchangeably, although software worker usually refers to a more inclusive category than programmer.

associated with edp, is both terse and highly descriptive. The sequence of instructions which controls the machine is called the "program;" the people who produce the programs are called, logically, "computer programmers." Given this, it would seem easy enough to go on and say with reasonable accuracy how many programmers there are, how and where they are trained, who works where, and under what conditions they labor. As it happens, we can't. The problem is that the work of providing instructions to the computer is no longer done only by people called computer programmers. To confirm this, open any big-city newspaper to the want-ads section for computer specialists. There are literally dozens of job titles and descriptions listed, ranging from programmers in various applied specializations ("financial programmer," "production control specialist"), and such exotic jobs as "real-time systems programmer/communications" and "COBOL operating systems programmer," to such impressive, if vague, titles as "systems analyst" and "systems engineer," and "Management Information Consultant." Hardly anywhere to be found is the plain, unadorned "computer programmer."

What the want-ads tell us, most obviously, is that programmers are employees rather than independent entrepreneurs, and they are employed in an impressive variety of workplaces to do an impressive number of jobs.[3] The nature and number of programming suboccupations varies greatly from industry to industry, organization to organization, and even within the same organization. Furthermore, the suboccupations (often qualified by such ranks as "senior," "associate," "junior," etc.) are being constantly redefined. So many different jobs arranged in an ever-shifting hierarchy make any analysis of programmers and their work—or even a simple headcount of the people in the field—a very confusing business unless some precautions are taken. What may be true of people at the bot-

---

[3] The want-ads do not and cannot tell us that some software workers work at something else for a living in spite of their official job titles. For the most part, these are salespeople and managers; their inclusion in the general category of "software worker" is largely a convenient fiction, useful for inflating an organization's technical staff when competing for contracts and sales. On the other hand, there are many employees who are officially classified as typists or machine operators (and are so reported in census tabulations) who in fact regularly program as part of their jobs. Because of the gender difference between managerial, sales, and clerical workers, most of the nonprogramming "programmers" are men, while many of the programming "nonprogrammers" are women. See p. 106.

tom of the organizational ladder may be only partly true of those on the top—or not true at all.[4]

Given all this, I have divided software workers into three broad categories, defined by both the nature of their work and their social relations in the software workplace. Briefly, they are

(1) *Coders*. Coders do the least "creative" part of programming: the tedious, slow work of writing down the symbols (the "code;" hence the name) which express the program. Code is the "alphabet" of a programming "language" and the tendency in the industry is to assign coders a role and a status resembling those of clerks, to whom they are increasingly compared. There is room for some individual decision making here, but it is limited and under constant pressure to conform to standardized procedures of coding. Coders are the "grunts" of programming, the bottom of the ladder.

(2) *Programmers*. Programmers are given an edp problem (which may be specific or general) and create a program to solve it. They generally work on all aspects of program production: design, writing (coding), debugging, and final writing, although in many workplaces programmers are divided into functional groups, some specializing in design, others in debugging, still others in documentation, i.e., compiling an inventory of a program's logic, goals, components, etc. Sometimes programmers do their own coding, sometimes parts are done for them by coders.

---

[4] The 1970 Census gave approximately a quarter of a million as the number of "computer specialists," a term which included programmers, systems analysts, and a third, catch-all, group. The breakdown was

Job Category	Male	Female	Total
Computer programmer	124,956	36,381	161,337
Computer systems analyst	68,213	11,736	79,949
Computer programmers n.e.c.	11,445	1,806	13,251
Totals	204,614	49,923	254,537

(From United States Department of Commerce, Bureau of the Census. *Census of the Population, 1970. United States, Detailed Characteristics*, p. 725.)

This can at best be an informed guess. In 1973 I was told by a member of a special National Bureau of Standards panel on programmers that, as far as they were able to calculate, the number of software workers in the United States was "somewhere between a quarter of a million and a million," a vagueness which reflects less the Bureau's inability to count than its inability to decide what a programmer is. Figures for British software workers can be found in Ward.

Their work, while considerably more varied and autonomous than that of coders, still involves a great deal of routine detail work.

(3) *Systems Analysts*. Analysts are generally responsible for designing whole, complex data processing systems rather than parts of larger ones as programmers do. As a result, they tend more than the other two software workers to be "customer's men," go-betweens as much as technical specialists. Their position is especially ambiguous because their work contains elements of the manager and salesman as well as the technical expert. It represents in microcosm the internal conflicts present in many engineering, technical, and scientific organizations.

As they are described here, the groupings clearly overlap—everyone does at least some coding, for example. This is deliberate: it is meant to suggest the practice which characterizes real edp workplaces and which is formalized in the common job titles meant to indicate intermediate positions. The term "programmer/coder," for example, is often applied to people who primarily code although they may also do some analytical work. "Programmer/analyst," on the other hand, indicates a programmer may also do some large-scale work on the "architecture" of a software system.

In spite of the lack of clear-cut boundaries between the software suboccupations, the divisions point to what may be the most important aspect of modern programming: the work of head and hand have been separated and given over to different people. The divisions as they are outlined on pp. 15–16, constitute a sequence ranging from routine work that involves relatively little thought, to the most far-reaching conceptualization and definition of what problems are to be solved by computers and how, i.e., the basic decisions which in our society are usually reserved for owners, executives, or managers. We can see this reflected in the relatively sparse[5] literature on

---

[5] Given the enormous importance of computers and the people who make them work, there is surprisingly little written about software workers by social scientists. Much more has been written about the effects of edp on nonsoftware workers, especially clericals, e.g., Hoos (1961), or on production workers, e.g., Blauner. On the other hand, management literature abounds. Most of it, predictably, is concerned with how managers can get programmers to do what they want them to.

Of the few social scientists writing on programmers, the most notable are Hebden, Mumford, and Meyer. A short account of the programming specialists attached to the World War II machines is found in Goldstine.

A study which stradles the line between management tract and insightful survey of the software workplace is Gerald M. Weinberg's unfortunately titled

software workers, which tends to divide programmers into just two groups, one made up of coders and some applications programmers, the other of analytical/managerial specialists. A study of automation in the workplace by Jon Shepard provides a recent sociological example:

> . . . personnel performing software functions are a new type of office employee. . . . it is most logical to consider their functions to be "clerical." They are, to be sure, a novel type of clerical employee, being one of the automated man-machine relationships created by computer technology. (Shepard, pp. 61–62)[6]

He acknowledges a major discrepancy in this assessment, however—the matter of pay:

> In the large insurance company participating in this study, programmers and systems analysts are in middle management in terms of salary level, but their actual duties are neither supervisory nor managerial. In fact, advanced computer operators, if placed by salary level, would also be classified as managerial. (p. 61)

To Shepard, the anomaly between status, function, and pay is largely a matter of newness, a confusion which will disappear as programmers are adapted into existing workplace organizations and structures.

The more complex work of systems design and analysis has been examined by a British researcher, John Hebden. Unlike Shepard, who studied software workers as only one of several "office" occupations, Hebden examines software employees as a special case, and in particular, the differences in work between programmers and analysts. He concludes that the two

---

The Psychology of Computer Programming. Programming, of course, does not have a psychology, although programmers usually do. The title is representative of a widespread tendency to anthropomorphize the field and even the machines. The book, in any case, is indispensable.

There is, finally, a separate though related literature on "futurologists," some of it laudatory and enthusiastic, most of it highly critical. See Hoos (1974) and Boguslaw, for two knowledgeable and generally unimpressed assessments.

[6] People, of course, create relations between each other and between themselves and the machines they make, not the other way around. To say, as Shepard does, that man-machine relations are created by computer technology is to go beyond the realm of social analysis into the realm of an "engineering without people" or mysticism or—as so often happens—both. Here, Shepard succumbs to a common tendency to mystify technology and give it a life of its own, independent of the people who create it and the people who use it. Shepard's methodology, in which the nature of the work is used to define the social relations of the workplace, must inevitably lead him to the conclusion that the dog is wagged by the tail.

are emerging as distinct occupations because they do different kinds of work. Coders and programmers fill in the details, while systems analysts design the architecture of a program and set specifications to be met in writing them. Along with Shepard, he considers the classification of software specialists in general a relatively straightforward affair: they are either clericals or they are the people who provide them with the clerical tasks to be done (Hebden).[7]

In spite of its popularity among academic researchers, this is a perspective largely borrowed from managers, who find it useful for their own reasons to divide software workers into clerks and managers of clerks.[8] There is, however, so wide a range of skills, job content, and hierarchical position among software workers that to call them simply clericals or managers is to ignore the genuine complexity of their work as well as the ambiguity of their relations to both managers and production workers.

Programmers as engineers

A different approach, which emphasizes both the technical component of their work and their ambiguous social role, defines software workers at all levels as offshoots of engineering workers. Put in a slightly different way, programmers are looked at as technical employees rather than clerical workers who may also have some technical (or management) skills. The distinction, a basic one, needs elaboration because labeling anyone an engineer seems to narrow rather than enlarge an

---

[7] Hebden goes somewhat further than Shepard in approaching the matter of social relations and workplace control:

. . . although there is an overlap in the area of systems and programming specification, control of this area of activity is the subject of further argument and dispute. . . . For the systems analyst, the client is the user group in whose area he is working or the senior management whose objectives are going to be furthered by the implementation of the system. For the programmer, the ultimate user is remote and the immediate client is in fact the systems analyst who has prepared the specification and who will receive the completed package in order that the system may be tested. (p. 15)

For the most part, though, Hebden is concerned with either the job content of the various software occupations or the subjective differences in aspirations, career plans, and attitudes of software workers towards employers, jobs, and their occupation.

[8] The perspective is a variant of the so-called job-enlargement school, of which the best-known academic representatives are Robert Blauner and William Faunce. Typically, job-enlargement proponents define the role of workers by the content of their work rather than by the social relations of the workplace. Thus, because most programmers, i.e., coders and low-level applications programmers, are usually employed to do something called "information processing," they can be labelled clerks rather than technical specialists. The simple act of defining them as clerical workers gives managers a psychological weapon in their efforts to push software workers down a corporate hierarchy.

individual's social role. The confusion stems from a popular but misleading stereotype of the history and function of modern engineering. Although the engineer's role in the American production process has usually been thought of in exclusively technical terms, it has in fact been considerably broader and more inclusive. Since their emergence at the end of the 19th century,[9] modern engineers have been employed by owners and managers to redesign work processes in order to make them amenable to standardization. Their job was to break down other people's jobs into subtasks, each of which required less skill to perform than the original whole job which they collectively replaced. To the extent the engineers succeeded, much work formerly done by skilled labor could be transferred to less skilled workers or even to machines. In the latter case, engineers logically went further and designed, built, and improved the machines which replaced human labor. Engineers thus became the instruments with which managers effected, in Harry Braverman's phrase, the separation of the conception of work from its execution. Conception, of course, was to be reserved for managers, while execution was assigned to production workers. Engineers, in effect, were the skilled experts called upon by their employers to make other employees less skilled and less expert.[10]

It should be stressed that the head/hand separation was not (and is not) the division between an entrepreneur's decision to make a product and the actual task of making it. Obviously, such distinctions had been around long before engineers or mass-production engineering industries. What *was* new was the conscious desire of managers to directly oversee every aspect of the actual production process (Stone). Managerial efforts in that direction began in earnest at the turn of the present century. Only in part were they prompted by a concern with efficiency in the strict economic sense, that is, getting more output for the same or less input. Another concern, quite plainly voiced by proponents of the new Scientific Manage-

[9] Much of the following discussion as well as the discussion of electrical engineers in Chapter 2 is based on David Noble's important work, *America by Design: Science, Technology and the Rise of Corporate Capitalism.* A shorter history of engineering in the United States is in Edwin Layton's "Science, Business, and the American Engineer," in Robert Perrucci and Joel Gerstl, Eds., *The Engineers and the Social System.* The latter volume is in general a very useful one.

[10] Harry Braverman's *Labor and Monopoly Capital: The Degradation of Work in the Twentieth Century,* has, perhaps more than any other single book, revived interest in work and occupations among social scientists in the United States. The present work has been greatly influenced by Braverman's insistence that shifts within occupations are as crucial as shifts between them. In a field as new as programming, Braverman's advice is especially relevant.

ment school,[11] was *control*. When engineers broke down a product's manufacture into the smallest possible component parts, employers needed fewer skilled production workers. Quite apart from whatever lowering of labor costs might result, reducing skill levels gave employers a great advantage because it reduced their dependence on a few critical employees who might strike or simply go elsewhere for better terms. It meant, furthermore, that much of the production process could be given over to machines which had almost none of the disadvantages of human labor (a general unreliability, legal restrictions on hours and conditions of employment and labor, a tendency to form unions, etc.) and only one serious disadvantage of their own: employers couldn't lay off machines during slack times.

Engineers thus played not one but two major roles in the workplace and both had distinct social shadings in addition to being simply "technical":

(1) They *rearranged and redesigned* work tasks in order to increase managerial control over the production process at the expense of production workers.

(2) They *simplified* work tasks to the extent that some could be done by less skilled workers or by (engineer-designed) machines.

The result was to reduce the scope of production workers' activities, reduce their average skill levels, and intensify the division between managers who did the thinking and production workers who did everything else. Engineers, then, are considerably more than technical specialists: not managers themselves, they are extensions of management in the way a tool is an extension of a craftsman.

In this sense, computer programmers are the ultimate engineers. Their work has been used to make possible the application of what is the most spectacular of all machines designed to do routine work or—which is not quite the same thing—to do work tasks which have been made routine. Telephone operators, to recall an earlier example, have been more or less eliminated except for nonroutine calls (e.g., assistance) as have the old-fashioned billings clerks from everywhere except the smallest establishments. Nowadays, such applications are simple stuff for computers, and machine-controlled or

---

[11] The Scientific Management movement occupies a critical place in the history of American industry. Its founder and for many years its most forceful spokesman was Frederick W. Taylor, who also gave his name to the movement. Braverman thinks Taylorism was never really replaced by the newer "human relations" approach to personnel management, but simply reappeared in various guises using more fashionable techniques as covers. This is, I think, overstating the case, but the Taylorist emphasis on absolute workplace control persists.

machine-assisted work is done in the most diverse settings. Programmers have been able to use advanced hardware to carry out complicated production processes formerly done by skilled machinists (through a process called numerical control). Automobile, rail, and even air traffic increasingly are regulated by electronic data processing machines instead of policemen or railroad dispatchers or air controllers. Typists have been giving way to automated "word processing" equipment. These, it should be stressed, are only the less exotic examples of the trend. Such drastic changes in how work is done—and by whom—have come about because managers and owners have assigned software specialists the task of finding work which involves any sort of routine, repetitive activity that can be standardized and then done in a standard, i.e., machine-controlled, manner.

Are programmers, then, "a novel type of clerical employee" or the technical "point men" for managers in the tradition of other engineers? The answer is that some software workers are primarily engineers, while others are high-powered clericals. To label all of them clericals (or clerical managers) is to say that programming involves no technical skill—which is obviously not true—as well as to deny its use as a de-skilling tool. Similarly, lumping all software workers together as quasimanagerial engineers ignores a major fact of life for all engineering employees in American society. What some of them have done to de-skill production workers, other engineers will do to them in the same way and for the same reasons. Engineers are constantly seeing their own training, skills, and work roles labeled "obsolete" as a result of the work done by their own colleagues.[12] The history of American

---

[12] The phenomenon of the short career line for engineers is well known. If engineers don't move into management or sales ten years or so after their last engineering degree, they run a serious risk of being laid off for "obsolescence." There is some disagreement whether it is the older engineer's skills or salary that employers consider obsolete, a discussion which applies to programmers as well. See pp. 82–83. See also Fischer and Lesser.

It bears mentioning, too, that for some reason a lot of people who write about engineering workers don't seem to like them very much. The attitude is nonpartisan. Management writers barely disguise their contempt, calling engineers narrowly specialized, money-grubbing cretins. What they say in private management conferences is even less flattering. Radical critics, who might be expected to show more sympathy for the engineering worker, rake them over for mindlessly performing work harmful to people, the environment, peace, etc. Both are playing slightly different versions of a popular game called blaming the victim for the villain. The confusion was first expressed by Thorstein Veblen in his *Engineers and the Price System,* published during World War I. His comments then about how easy it is to buy off engineers with a "full dinner pail" have been uncritically accepted ever since by managers and radical critics alike. Perhaps the most notable among the latter is Herbert Marcuse, who added Freud to Veblen and got "repressive tolerance."

engineering is quite clear about this and explains why, unlike the European experience, engineers are vastly outnumbered by "technicians." In a similar way, programming has been subjected to the same kind of analysis, restructuring, division and subdivision of labor and control as every other engineering work. The result has been a rank-ordering of the major suboccupations: clerical-like software workers (primarily coders) on the bottom, problem-defining analysts/managers on the top, and a goodly number of people in ambiguous positions scattered in between. The gap between top and bottom, not to say the confusion of those in the middle, increases daily.

This is only one of many such paradoxes we will encounter as we proceed. Programmers, systems analysts, and other software workers are experiencing efforts to break down, simplify, routinize, and standardize their own work so that it, too, can be done by machines instead of people. Computers are the most sophisticated instruments available to managers in their efforts to de-skill production workers and now they are being used against the very people who made it possible for managers to so use them. Elaborate efforts are being made to develop ways of gradually eliminating programmers, or at least reduce their average skill levels, required training, experience, and so on. The most important of these—software development and workplace structure—are examined in subsequent chapters. The first place to look at the trend is not in programming itself, however, but in the development of the machine.

The computer and how it grew

This is a study of computer programmers, not of computing machines. A complete, thorough history of computing hardware obviously can't be undertaken here.[13] But programmers exist only because they have computers to program and therefore it is necessary to know something of how the hardware developed into its present form. It is especially necessary because present-day computers have evolved as a result of industry efforts to rid itself of its dependence on highly skilled software specialists and replace them with a coalition of a few "software scientists" and a much larger number of machine operators and clerks.

The first machines

If the physicians or auto mechanics or school teachers who learned their trades 50 or even 30 years ago are sometimes

[13] Useful histories of the World War II machines are found in Hollingdale and Toothill and Rosen. See also Goldstine. All describe the considerable contributions British specialists made during the war, something I have not been able to do here.

astounded by the current states of their fields, each of them is still able to recognize the form, substance, and social role of their respective occupations. The same, however, cannot be said of computer specialists. The first modern computers—ENIAC, produced by the Moore School of Electrical Engineering of the University of Pennsylvania, and the Mark I, produced at Harvard University—were World War II projects funded largely by the military. They were intended primarily to help calculate shell trajectories, although ENIAC also aided in the computations for the nuclear bomb project at Los Alamos. Both were essentially giant collections of registers. By modern standards they were exceedingly clumsy devices, composed largely of electromechanical or electrical switches regulated by vacuum tubes. Quantities to be calculated by the machines were fed into them on paper or magnetic tape or punched cards. Changes in the operating "program" were made by adjusting a given combination of switches and physically rearranging special self-contained circuits called "plug boards." These were circuits permanently wired to perform specific calculations such as square roots or cosines and were "plugged in" or removed as needed. The entire cumbersome process was known as "external programming" since the instructions could be changed only by physically moving the plug boards, control switches, etc.

External programming was a tedious and inefficient enterprise, since even minor programming changes required that part of the machine be, in effect, rewired. In addition, a given set of instructions—the program—had to be absolutely complete before the machine could do so much as add a column of numbers. Someone had to anticipate which of the machine's many circuits would be used and the order of their use, and then had to make sure the instructions themselves were correctly entered in the proper sequence. Finally—and this was the most tedious and time-consuming of all—the program contained on tape or cards had to be entered in a form the machine was able to accept and act on. Providing the computer with instructions in this manner was in many respects an exercise in a complex kind of electrical engineering. Plug boards helped reduce somewhat the need for step by step, circuit by circuit programming, but the overwhelming mass of "machine language" programming still had to be done, slowly and ever prone to error, by human programmers.

The disadvantages of this sort of programming were well understood from the start. The machine, assuming it did not break down, could process numeric information much more quickly than its users could prepare the operating instructions

and feed it numbers to process. The skills needed to program
the machine were esoteric, not easily learned, and less easily
mastered, not to mention time-consuming and subject to the
most common kind of clerical error. The chief complaint
against the computer, in fact, was not against the primitive
hardware itself, but the limitations of the people who used it. It
is a complaint still being made today.

The stored program computer

Even as the ENIAC computer was being put into operation, its
creators were working to replace it with machines which could
be programmed and used in less painstaking, time-consuming
ways. The first major step in this direction was the introduction
of the so-called "stored program" computer in the late
1940s.[14] The concept is relatively simple in theory and all
modern computers are still based on its principles. The instructions which operate the machine are stored in the machine's
"memory" along with the data to be processed. A hardware
control unit within the main body of the computer (called the
"central processor") decodes the stored instructions and
causes the computer's arithmetic and logic units to process the
data.

At first, these instructions were written in "machine-
language," a form of binary code that is extraordinarily complex and difficult to prepare. It was not long before easier ways
to write programs—sets of instructions—were developed.
Symbolic "source" languages were created in which instructions were written in alphabetic and decimal code. The computers themselves could be used (when properly programmed)
to translate the source code into machine-language. This was,
of course, a great saving of time as well as a major step toward
simplification of programming. The development of symbolic
code languages relieved the "applications programmer" of
having to write instructions in machine language, in fact, from
having to know machine language or to understand much at all
about the machine.

It must be emphasized that the reduction in programming
complexity and tedium made possible by the stored program
computer did not come about because *all* programming had

---

[14] There is a long-standing debate in the computer world over who "invented"
the stored-program machine, or rather, who first thought of the concept. According to one's preference, the honor goes either to John von Neumann or to
J. P. Eckert and J. W. Mauchly, all colleagues on the Moore School ENIAC
project. The dispute, as one might anticipate, was not simply one of scientific
priority; involved were the rights to patents which would prove crucial to the
commercial exploitation of the new machine. Opposite sides in the dispute are
presented by Goldstine and Rosen.

been simplified. On the contrary, for a minority of programmers the job got even more elaborate and tedious. The stored program computer made programming easier for some software workers only because others now had to do a much more involved and time-consuming kind of programming. Machine language programs, far from being replaced by the new machines, were being written in greater number than ever before; and added to the task of writing them was the equally time-consuming and detailed job of writing the so-called "processors" that mediated between source code programs and machine-language instructions. The more simplified the source code (or the more elaborate the computer application or both), the more complex and time-consuming were the required machine language instructions and translator. The advantage—and it is a great one—was that much programming could now be done using the simpler source code to get the machine to do what was wanted.

The essential paradox of the computer—its ability to operate more quickly than the ability of its human creators to use it—was thus partially resolved only by intensifying it. The machine's operation was made even more complex and required even greater skill and time on the part of some specialists to make it work, but once the complex operating software was written and installed, many more people with relatively fewer software skills could use the machine.

Later developments

The idea of the stored program computer coincided with another watershed invention, the transistor. Together, they made possible more reliable machines which could process more numbers more quickly than ever before while reducing the machine's bulk and operating costs. In turn, this made possible the application of the machine's dull but dependable calculation skills to new and more complex areas. The trend was accelerated by other technological and engineering advances. Chief among these was the development of microcircuits, which in turn contributed to the process of further hardware miniaturization. The major consequence of these technological developments is that the machines have gotten steadily more complex and elaborate and their application extended into areas undreamed of by the developers of the original World War II machines. Consider the following comparison. The computations performed by ENIAC (which occupied an entire floor and required 18,000 vacuum tubes as well as the constant attention of programmers and machine operators) can today be done more quickly and more cheaply by a computer only a little larger than an electric typewriter—and in fact such computation would not be considered much of a test of the newer machine's capabilities.

Hardware miniaturization meant much more than a reduction of the machine's size. It also meant that the original benefits of the stored program principle could be expanded almost indefinitely. Whole "libraries" of special routines could be stored in relatively small auxilliary units and called for when needed without significantly reducing the machine's core (i.e., data) memories or slowing down the central processor. The technique, known as microprogramming, made it possible to do common processing problems (such as bookkeeping reports) by using the simplest possible code. Again, our bank teller is a handy example, but the principle was soon applied to much more elaborate applications. Software specialists soon developed a series of powerful "high-level" programming languages which could generate extensive and complicated machine operations when requested to do so in the most economical source code. Specialized languages such as FORTRAN (*FOR*mula *TRAN*slator) for mathematical and scientific applications, COBOL (*CO*mmon *B*usiness *O*riented *L*anguage) for commercial and financial applications, PL/I (*P*rogramming *L*anguage/*I*) which combined aspects of both, as well as others like APL and BASIC were created and put into widespread use in short order.

Separation of user and programmer

With the exception of time-sharing,[15] the advances which came after solid-state technology, microprogramming, and so on, have been primarily on the order of refinements rather than radical transformations. Hardware innovations and the high-level programming languages which they made possible had taken their essential form by the middle of the 1960s, even though some of them took many years more to be widely adopted. Since then, emphasis in the hardware industry has been to devise ways to simplify existing technology and expand its application to areas formerly considered too involved for machines. This, after all, was what computing was supposed to be about: to free people from the petty details of hand calculation so they could use their time and imagination to formulate problems or devise uses for the solutions.

But *which* people? For all but the most straightforward ap-

---

[15] Time-sharing is a software technique which orders the sequence in which the programs of unrelated users are entered and processed by the same machine. The computer can be instructed to process some of the data of one user, then some of another, and so on, returning to each in a determined order. Because it does so very fast, there is for each individual user no noticeable interruption in his data processing and he interacts with it as if he had sole use of the machine. This, of course, increases the effective capacity of the computer enormously.

plications, the skills required for competent, efficient programming were becoming increasingly involved and time-consuming. Many programming tasks were simply beyond the skills of the casually trained, occasional user. Certainly, writing machine-code or translators was a demanding full-time job. As applications expanded, the "computer specialist" soon became many specialists, classified in the same way as other technical employees, both by function (e.g., software design, coding), and the nature of the work (numerical control, bookkeeping/accounting, scientific/mathematical, software development, systems languages, etc.), as well as social role and position (software production, customer relations, management, etc.).

In short, expanding applications and increasing complexity combined to require the services of people skilled in the ways computers worked rather than in the substance and content of their application. Responsibility for the computer's operation had been transferred to a new, or rather, several new, specialized occupations. The "final users"—primarily large organizations which could afford the hardware—became the employers of skilled workers, who, like some other employees, operated advanced labor-saving machines. This has proved to be quite important. The desire of organizational users to treat computers like other labor-saving machinery intensified the already great pressure on hardware makers to simplify the computer's use. The goal, expressed early and often in the short history of the computer, is the same as in all other engineering industries: managerial control. In 1959, at a symposium sponsored by the Systems Development Corporation (a RAND Corporation spin-off), Robert Bosak, a consultant in edp management, put the matter quite clearly:

> Progress in all of these areas of [software] research have important implications for management control systems. In the area of programming language, developments will make it possible for programs to be written and modified more efficiently both from the standpoints of manhours and elapsed time required. It will also make it possible for less highly trained personnel to program the computer. The ultimate is to remove the programmer entirely from the process of writing operational programs. In effect, the manager would write and modify his own programs. (Bosak, pp. 212–213)[16]

[16] Bosak's description is somewhat misleading. Programmers could not and cannot yet be completely eliminated, no matter how fervently their employers wished it so. What Bosak had in mind was a software system (and suitable hardware) so complete and so thoroughly "wired in" that virtually anyone could "talk" to a computer and get from it what was wanted. Of course, for this to be done requires the very greatest programming skills and talent—greater than any yet demonstrated.

Bosak and other management consultants did not really anticipate the elimination of *all* programmers, only the replacement of most applications programmers and coders by an alliance of the most advanced computer scientists on the one hand and nonprogrammers, such as managers or clerks, on the other. Although the managerial vision has yet to be realized, hardware producers have made impressive advances to bring the day closer. Ten years after the SDC conference, a computer scientist was able to summarize the accomplishments of the decade:

The fundamental result of the development in this period was that "computer systems" no longer meant hardware alone. The system which the programmer used had both hardware and [built-in] software components, and it was not always possible or necessary for him to distinguish whether a specific function was accomplished by one or the other. (Rosin, p. 47)

In such computer systems, it is unnecessary for the programmer to distinguish between a function that is "wired into" the machine and one which another programmer entered, perhaps years ago, e.g., the writer of the assembler or the systems programmer who helped design the machine's operating system. The most striking effects of this functional merging of hardware and software are seen in the work of the so-called applications programmer. These are software workers who use high-level languages like COBOL or PL/I to solve carefully defined and structured problems, e.g., payroll accounting or inventory control, and who need only rudimentary programming skills compared to those of the small number of software specialists who designed the languages they use. Those same languages (which now have specialized "dialects" that are still simpler to use in limited-purpose applications) make it possible for some final users, that is, managers and nonsoftware technical specialists, to deal directly with the machine in an increasing number of areas—without making use of the help of applications programmers at all.

Most of the people we have called programmers, in short, have been relegated largely to subsidiary and subordinate roles in the production process. They are technicians and engineers who preside over the latest variety of labor-saving machinery, whose use and purpose are specifically excluded from their job responsibilities. While a few of them sit at the side of managers, counselling and providing expert's advice, most simply carry out what someone else has assigned them.

Machines should work, proclaims an IBM advertisement, people should think. The computer was supposed to be the instrument to accomplish this happy division of machine-man labor. Yet, so far, only a select minority formulate problems, make the decisions, and take appropriate action based on information provided by the computer. Most of the routine and tedium associated with the daily tasks of producing programs are left to an anonymous army of people who merely do what they are told, understanding little of what they do and less of why they are doing it. At least up to now, the computer has intensified, not reduced, the separation between those who think and those who do everything else, a division now beginning to separate software workers as well.

References   Blauner, Robert (1964). *Alienation and Freedom*. Chicago: University of Chicago Press.

Boguslaw, Robert (1965). *The New Utopians: A Study of Systems Design and Social Change*. Englewood Cliffs, N.J.: Prentice-Hall.

Bosak, Robert (1960). Implications of computer programming research for management controls. In Malcolm and Rowe.

Braverman, Harry (1974). *Labor and Monopoly Capital: The Degradation of Work in the Twentieth Century*. New York and London: Monthly Review Press.

Faunce, William (1958). Automation in the automobile industry. *Am. Soc. R.* 23:401–407.

Fischer, Britta, and Mary Lesser (1973). Engineers. *Science for the People*. V, 3:16–21.

Goldstine, Herman (1972). *The Computer: From Pascal to Von Neumann*. Princeton: Princeton University Press.

Hebden, J. E. (1974). Patterns of work identification. Salford, England: University of Salford (mimeo).

Hollingdale, S. H., and G. C. Toothill (1965). *Electronic Computers*. Baltimore: Penguin Books.

Hoos, Ida (1961). *Automation in the Office*. Washington: Public Affairs Press.

Hoos, Ida (1974). *Systems Analysis in Public Policy: A Critique*. Berkeley and Los Angeles: University of California Press.

Layton, Edwin (1969). Science, business, and the American engineer. In Perrucci and Gerstl.

Malcolm, D. G., and A. J. Rowe (1960). *Management Control Systems*. New York: John Wiley & Sons.

Meyer, Marshall (1968). Automation and the bureaucratic structure. *Am. J. Soc.* 74,3:256–264.

Mumford, Enid (1972). *Job Satisfaction: A Study of Computer Specialists*. London: Longman.

Noble, David (1977). *America by Design: Science, Technology and The Rise of Corporate Capitalism*. New York: Knopf (forthcoming).

Perrucci, Robert, and Joel Gerstl (1969). *The Engineers and the Social System*. New York: John Wiley & Sons.

Rosen, Saul (1969). Electronic computers: a historical survey. *Computing Surveys* I, 1:7–36.

Rosin, Robert (1969). Supervisory and monitor systems. *Computing Surveys* I, 1:37–54.

Shepard, Jon (1971). *Automation and Alienation: A Study of Office and Factory Workers*. Cambridge: MIT Press.

Stone, Katherine (1973). The origins of job structure in the steel industry. *Radical America* VII, 6:19–64.

Ward, Tom (1973). *Computers, Organisation, Personnel and Control*. London: Longman.

Weinberg, Gerald M. (1971). *The Psychology of Computer Programming*. New York: Van Nostrand Reinhold.

2 The organization of formal training

The engineering heritage and its consequences Nowhere is the head/hand separation among software workers or its social impact better illustrated than in the way software training is organized. Although formal training, acquired in institutions specifically established for that purpose, is still new and largely *ad hoc,* it would be wrong to assume that it has been entirely without precedent. In fact, the training of software workers has followed a surprisingly well-worn path, particularly in light of the science-fiction aura of the machines. The relative newness of computing machines should not be allowed to obscure an important fact: computers were and continue to be made by electrical engineers, people with a long tradition of making similar, if less glamorous, machines. The original ENIAC and Mark I were electrical or electromechanical counting devices—who other than electrical engineers could have been better suited to design and build them?

Reasonably enough, the training of computer specialists, including software specialists, developed initially as a subdivision of electrical engineering and thus borrowed from its traditions. The heritage has proved pivotal.[1] Although it is often assumed that twentieth-century engineering occupations, including electrical engineering, are continuations of the older civil and mechanical engineering, in fact old and new share little except the title. In both their work and social position, the 18th and 19th century builders of roads and canals and managers of factories resembled present-day small entrepreneurs

---

[1] The discussion of electrical engineering, its relation to the electrical industry, and its role as model for other engineering occupations is substantially taken from Noble.

and managers more than the technical specialists we now call engineers. Modern engineers, unlike their namesakes, were from their beginnings the creations and creatures of the industries which employed them. They were designed to be employees, in other words, not small owners or managers. "Designed" seems appropriate because engineers of the new type, who began to appear in substantial numbers by the 1880s, were produced and used in much the same way as other industrial products were produced and used.[2] They were conceived and employed, in David Noble's apt phrase, to wed the sciences and the useful arts in the service of America's electrical and chemical industries which together made up the leading edge of America's burgeoning science-based industries. Workers were selected, recruited, and put to work appropriating scientific advances to help solve the practical problems of large-scale industrial production and, not incidentally, to increase corporate profitability. They were considered by their employers to be another raw material, much as the metals or minerals used to fashion electric generators or chemical dyestuffs.

Raw materials or not, engineers were not to be had just by digging them out of the ground. They had to be trained. From the 1890s to the end of World War I, leaders of the electrical and other engineering industries carried on a well-organized and well-financed campaign to promote technical training at all levels of public and private education. While corporations individually and through industry associations subsidized selected private institutions (including the Massachusetts Institute of Technology, Antioch College, and Rensselaer Polytechnical Institute), their goal was a vastly expanded national program of technical education, underwritten by federal and local governments and using the federal land-grant colleges both as precedent for and foundation of the proposed system.

World War I proved to be a watershed in their efforts. Pressure to increase industrial production, now happily spurred by patriotism as well as the profit motive, provided the incentive to collapse whatever distinctions remained between large-scale industry, government, and the American educational system. By war's end, a two-tier educational structure had been built which promised to supply corporations with the kind of engineering and technical workers they wanted. The first was supervised by the science-based industries themselves. En-

---

[2] The "worker as product" heritage of electrical engineering is sometimes expressed explicitly by management and academic researchers. Note, for example, the title of a 1972 article by John Hamblen, "Production and Utilization of Computer Manpower in U.S. Higher Education."

compassing classroom as well as on the job instruction, it was designed for narrow training and not, in most cases, to produce broadly educated, state-of-the-art scientific specialists. Instead, corporate schools concentrated on training workers who had little other formal education and who could be put into the production process months or even weeks after the start of company training. Such schools assured the firm of a steady supply of technically specialized workers who would learn only what the company wanted them to learn, dispensing with "superfluous" material not immediately useful to the employer. On a less technical level, managers welcomed company schools as a handy way of exposing employees to the company "point of view" along with more conventional instruction. From this managers hoped to instill a sense of loyalty among their technical workers—or at the very least find and eliminate potential troublemakers. It was a perfectly logical development, therefore, when the National Association of Corporate Schools, founded in 1913 by representatives of General Electric, Westinghouse, Bell Telephone, Western Electric, Boston Edison, etc., changed its name after the war to the American Management Association.

In-house training added to the pool of technical workers. But the science-based industries depended on more than these relatively low-level technical employees. They needed broadly trained engineers and scientists as well in order to maintain the pace of scientific advance. Here the company schools were supplemented by the newly restructured system of higher education. What had been before 1880 isolated and marginal technical academies became by 1917 a growing system of elite engineering colleges and scientific research institutions, amply funded with corporate and public money.[3] Even bastions of the classical curriculum like Harvard and Yale—which had as a matter of scholarly principle confined their science offerings to mathematics and perhaps a poorly equipped botany laboratory—established full-fledged science departments and even engineering schools.[4] A pattern of intimate cooperation

---

[3] "In the first decade following the passage of the Morrill [land grant college] Act, the number of engineering schools jumped from six to seventy. By 1880 there were 85 and by 1917 there were 126 engineering schools of college grade in the United States. Between 1870 and the outbreak of the First World War, the annual number of graduates from engineering colleges grew from 100 to 4300; the relative number of engineers in the whole population had multiplied fifteen-fold." (Noble, p. 24)

[4] Some elite liberal arts schools, however, couldn't quite bring themselves to go all the way. Harvard, for example, was given a substantial endowment to start an engineering school. Instead, it floated the money down the Charles to its sister institution, the Massachusetts Institute of Technology, which used the income until the benefactor's family found out and brought the matter to court.

was firmly established between technical institutions and the science-based industries—as well it should. The institutions owed their existence to the efforts of the industries and the industries needed the schools' graduates. It was a straightforward case of corporate demand and educational supply, a symbiotic relationship, the terms of which—financial and political support in return for a ''sensitivity'' to the personnel needs of industry—were well understood by both parties. (Smith, pp. 66–111)

By the 1920s the science-based industries had constructed for themselves a smoothly functioning system to produce loyal employees at several levels of technical skill. Narrowly trained technical workers—inevitably called ''technicians''—were instructed directly by the companies themselves in production skills and in an appreciation of the sacredness of corporate profitability. Higher-level engineering and scientific employees were trained by technical and engineering institutions and even in some traditional universities. As a result of careful admissions policies, the loyalty of these elite employees was assured, if not to a specific company, then at least to the corporate system as a whole. Selectively recruited, narrowly educated, and carefully indoctrinated to do exactly what their employers told them to do, engineers in the electrical industries (and their counterparts in other engineering occupations) were easily inserted into the recesses of rapidly expanding corporate bureaucracies. Even more than the gray-flanneled junior executives, they were the original company men.

Adapting tradition   There was, then, a poetic as well as a technical logic in electrical engineering's role in the development of the digital computer. The first systematic efforts to construct a computer, begining in the 1930s in university electrical engineering laboratories, marked what seemed to be the inevitable next step in the bureaucratization of the American workplace. Produced as a group effort and intended for massive data processing tasks, from a social as well as a technical point of view the computer was the ultimate product of electrical engineering. Electrical engineering itself had been one of the first technical occupations to undergo a process of systematic, corporate-defined bureaucratization. It was now to provide both the model and chief instrument in corporate efforts to standardize and routinize other occupations.

Once again, a war helped collapse the boundaries between the interests of the science-based industries, government, and the direction of American education. This time, the Second

World War did for the business machine industry what the First had done for the electrical and science-based industries as a whole. Directly or indirectly, the military underwrote virtually all the development costs of the new computing machines. It also underwrote the first efforts to develop systematic programming techniques and programmer instruction. No one had ever programmed before because there had never been computers before. The people who designed the circuitry of the military's new computers by necessity also designed the command system for the machines and passed on what they knew to their trainees and successors.[5] But it was obvious even before the ENIAC machine had performed its first official calculations early in 1946 that on the job training of programmers could turn out only a fraction of the people needed to operate the machines already being built. It was equally clear that if the infant computer industry was to prosper after the war, it would have to take measures to fill the gaps in the software workforce until a workable, conventionally organized training structure could be established. The efforts of the business machine industry to fill the gap can be divided into two periods, separated by the Korean War.

The early period: Hardware makers and in-house training.

Hardware makers were in a very good position to turn out machines almost as soon as the war was over, and commercial application of the computer took place with minimum delay. The quick transition from military to commercial production can be explained in part by the close relationship between military, corporate, and academic personnel. Two leaders of the Moore School (ENIAC) project, for example, J. P. Eckert and J. W. Mauchly, established their own firm a year or so after the war and by 1950 the company had become part of the Remington Rand (later Sperry Rand) Corporation. Harvard's Mark I, begun before the war, was built with the help of the International Business Machine Corporation. IBM supplied the Harvard laboratory with much of its equipment, materials, money, and engineering staff, reinforcing the long-standing ties between the company and project director, Dr. Howard Aiken.[6]

---

[5] This is, in any case, the account given in Goldstine. Goldstine was instrumental in bringing the military and the Moore School together in developing ENIAC. At the time of writing his history, he was an IBM fellow at that company's Yorktown Heights Research Facility. See also Chapter 3 of the present study.

[6] It should be added that IBM was actually slower than many others to undertake commercial production of computers. The delay was temporary, and IBM soon made up for lost time.

But if potential customers could get the hardware relatively quickly, getting programmers to run them was another matter. The solution, at least temporarily, was to produce software workers at the same time and in the same place as the hardware was turned out. The hardware makers really had little choice. They could not sell their machines unless there was a trained workforce to properly use them (although it should be pointed out that many of them tried anyway). Some turned necessity to advantage and treated their in-house-trained programmers as extensions of the company's salesforce. IBM, perhaps better than any of its competitors, understood that programmers trained by the company and using its machines would go out into the world carrying with them a profound appreciation of the virtues of IBM computers. Although IBM was not the first to manufacture large-scale, general purpose computers for commercial use (several others vie for the honor, the distinction probably belonging to the Eckert-Mauchly/Rand UNIVAC), they were the first to fully appreciate the wider social role of the programmer. It was that early insight which in part accounts for the company's domination of the present-day general purpose machine market. Their training courses, even by the standards of the electrical industry upon whose traditions they drew, were elaborate and carefully done. So prestigious was training acquired at "IBM school" during the 1950s and early 1960s, that government and private employers used the lure of IBM training to recruit potential employees in what was then a tight seller's market in programming.

Training by hardware makers during this period was supplemented—again, by necessity—with training offered by the users themselves. They, too, looked to the traditions of the electrical engineering industry and set up in-house training programs, combining classroom instruction (often with instructors loaned by thoughtful hardware makers) and on the job training. Training in these company[7] schools varied greatly according to the skills of the journeyman instructors, the hardware, the kinds of computation problems, as well as the capabilities of the students. As in the rest of the electrical industry, little time was spent on general or "theoretical" instruction; instead, efforts were directed towards training employees in skills immediately useful to the company, and

[7]Including, in case there is any confusion, the various and multiple government "shops." Prominent among these were the Navy, the Air Force, the Bureau of the Census, and the (National) Bureau of Standards, each critical backers and suppliers of development funds in the early days of the general purpose computer.

this, too, contributed to the diversity found in company school training.

Whatever the differences, however, all remained structured more or less along the same master/apprentice model developed during World War Two. It was at best a stop-gap measure and could not for long keep up with what even by the early 1950s was a frantic marketplace for computers and computer programmers. At this point, the software occupations began in a modest way to mimic the history of the parent industry.

The mass-production of programmers

The introduction of stored-program computers—1949 in England, a year later in the United States—made the task of quickly training software workers somewhat easier. The new machines standardized many of the software tasks required to make them work; training could now also be standardized more than it had been and thus more of it could take place in routinized settings, that is, in classrooms. Appropriately enough, it was once again a war which provided the incentive to organize the training of programmers in the same manner as other engineering occupations; and not surprisingly, it was the military which provided both the means and the setting to do so. The Cold War had culminated in the "police action" of Korea, and in America it produced a belief in an imminent Soviet air attack. In response, the United States government authorized the most elaborate of all edp projects the military (or anyone) had undertaken up to then—the Semi-Automatic Ground Environment, or SAGE. As the heart of an elaborate "early warning" radar network, SAGE was the first large-scale effort to use electronic data processors to make probability statements on the basis of huge quantities of changing data. SAGE's role in the history of software training came about because barely five years after the first computer went into service it undertook to train the 2,000 programmers necessary to make the project operational. Today, when programmers are as rare and exotic as, say, dentists, it is hard to appreciate the unprecedented demand for skilled workers this represented. To put the matter in perspective, one should consider that in 1950 there were perhaps no more than that number of programmers in the entire country. The 1950 census, in fact, did not even list them as an occupational category.

The task of doubling the national programmer workforce was given to the Systems Development Corporation (SDC), a spin-off of the RAND Corporation. SDC was asked to develop a crash training program, recruit whatever available

programmers could be found, increase their skills and provide
them with new ones, and make up the remaining manpower
deficit by training from scratch anyone it could recruit "off the
street." SDC managed to produce the required programmers;
it also produced much more.[8] Early in their training efforts,
SDC experts decided that the traditional master/apprentice
model of teaching people was slow, inefficient, and generated
a variety of undesirable "personnel problems." What were
needed were not new techniques to help people become programmers or to help programmers improve their ability to program. Instead, what was necessary was a series of *managerial
techniques* that would allow senior edp personnel to oversee
the activities and production of junior edp personnel. This was
a fundamental and, as it turned out, a far-reaching decision. It
represented the first systematic, large-scale effort on the part of
edp users to transform a highly idiosyncratic, artisan-like occupation into one which more closely resembled conventional
industrial work. That meant turning what had been almost
a handicraft activity into work whose pace, tools, and techniques, as well as organization and product, were controlled
by the "client" rather than the worker. It also meant that
the free-form work habits of individual programmers could
eventually be regularized, divided up, and then re-arranged
hierarchically along traditional bureaucratic production lines.

In short, a decision had been made by the largest employer
of software workers to create a whole class of managerial
employees to supervise the majority of programmer workers.
The "systems analyst," whose major function was to separate
programming tasks into less routine jobs (e.g., the overall
design of the solution to a dp problem) and more routine jobs
(e.g., coding), now began to appear with more frequency. In
effect, the SAGE/SDC program prompted the institutionaliza-
tion on a large-scale of the separation between the conception
of a computer program and the physical task of constructing it.
More to the point, it created the organizational divisions between the two, including the institutions designed to train one
or the other.

**Programming and
the academy**

By the end of the 1950s the analyst/coder separation developed
by SDC allowed the computer industry—manufacturers, users, and educators who served them both—to begin duplicat-
ing in the software occupations the time-tested structure of
engineering training pioneered by the electrical industry two

---

[8] For information about SAGE, I am grateful to Robert Boguslaw, now of
Washington University (St. Louis), one of the SDC "experts" who partici-
pated in the SAGE project. See also Hoos, p. 25.

generations before. The system is not yet as elaborate or as well-defined as the training structure of the parent industry. It is also in the middle of many and conflicting demands from hardware-makers, training institutions, users, and government agencies (the latter range from the Bureau of Standards to the Civil Rights Division of the Justice Department, as well as the ubiquitous military) who want software training to adjust or develop according to their particular needs or requirements. Nevertheless, the foundations of a functioning national system were firmly in place by 1970 and upon these have been built a familiar structure. It divides into two sections: a larger one which concentrates on coders and some applications programmers, and a second and much smaller which provides a few software specialists with broader and more intensive training.

Coders and some applications programmers are nowadays trained in-house (that is, after completing high school or equivalent training). Crossing the fuzzy line between coder and programmer (or programmer and analyst), however, means a general move from the corporate classroom to the academy. "Academy"-trained software workers make up a small part of the total programming workforce, just as formally trained engineers make up a small part of the technical workforce as a whole (Gilchrist and Weber, 1972a). They are specially trained to play a special role, largely in software research and development and in complex design work. Their distribution emphasizes the trend towards the separation of head and hand work: universities and scientific workplaces have the highest proportion, commercial and manufacturing applications the smallest, while engineering workplaces are generally in between.[9]

What is the nature of the programming academy? People familiar with the institutions that train programmers might ob-

---

[9] This can be only a general statement of relative distribution. There are no figures we can rely on for total number of software workers of all kinds (see Chapter 1, pp. 14–16 and footnotes 3 and 4), nor, obviously, for the education they received and how they are distributed by workplace. A few estimates have been made, using disparate and fragmentary information (Hamblen; Gilchrist and Weber, 1972a and 1972b). All concede they can offer only broad estimates of training trends.

The relative distribution among academic, engineering, scientific, and industrial workplaces described here reflects a consensus among managers, academics, and industrial consultants I have interviewed in connection with this study. It must be remembered, however, that the job tasks of software workers differ within each of these categories and so therefore will their training. For example, academic workplaces, such as computer centers or research laboratories, will employ low-level applications programmers as well as highly skilled technical specialists, while industrial workplaces (other than engineering industries) will employ highly trained systems people as well as coders, and so on.

ject to treating them all as a single type in view of their large number and great diversity. In fact, there are several very different kinds of programming academies, just as there are many different kinds of colleges and universities. A recent directory published by the Association for Computing Machinery (an important, if oddly titled, group we shall meet again) lists approximately 300 institutions, from the Pearl River Junior College in Poplarville, Mississippi, to Princeton, which have degree programs in software, data processing, or "computer science." The list, which represents nearly a sixth of all accredited post-high school educational institutions in the United States, inevitably understates both the extent and diversity of formal software training available today. It omits institutions which do not have separate degree programs in software training but which offer programming courses in other departments. It also overlooks, for whatever reason, others, like the Massachusetts Institute of Technology and the California Institute of Technology, which do offer degree programs.

Programmer-training institutions differ greatly, as do all educational institutions, particularly as we get closer to them. Anyone familiar with these institutions knows they are also prone to sudden, often drastic, changes in curriculum and focus, a state of affairs to be expected in a new field. In spite of their differences, however, programmer-training institutions constitute a coherent structure: while there are hundreds of institutions offering widely different programs and using different definitions of programmer and programming (as well as many more which offer edp courses on a less formal basis), they can be collected into just a few distinct groups. Apart from minor variations, within each group they share to an impressive degree notions of who is to receive what kind of software training and for whom they will work when their training is complete. The following, while it undoubtedly will hurt some academic feelings, describes the major subdivisions of the programmer "academy."

"Junior" engineering colleges and technical institutes

There are over 1000 community or "junior" colleges and two-year technical institutes in the United States, most of them publicly supported. Although not primarily programmer-training institutions, or for that matter, even exclusively technical in focus, most heavily emphasize vocational training. Training in data processing, electrical engineering, and some aspects of software has become popular in these institutions, although the level is usually basic. Indeed, a recent survey suggests that most formally trained programmers are trained in institutions such as these (Gilchrist and Weber, 1972a). Graduates may occasionally find jobs as programmers, but they are more likely to be hired as coders. In fact, as in the data processing "shops" where they eventually find work, software training is seen as an adjunct to machine operation; in practice most such "programmer" training is designed to be useful to people who will be in machine rooms operating the computer and peripheral equipment rather than somewhere else preparing programs.

Local employers play important direct roles in shaping curricula and course content. Junior colleges, as post-high school vocational institutions, are established to make local blue-collar youths more useful to local industry. They are then, by their nature, keenly aware of the labor requirements of large local employers and tailor their instruction accordingly. It is common for the instructional staff and the expert employees of local firms to overlap. Thus, machine room managers may teach on a part-time basis at a local community college, while college edp instructors may moonlight at the same firms. In a similar vein, colleges and local employers jointly establish work-study, intern, and summer employment programs which provide working class students with job experience. The same programs allow firms to evaluate the work habits, abilities, and attitudes of potential fulltime employees.[10]

Engineering and technical colleges

Engineering colleges represent a major transition from junior and community colleges both in terms of instructional level and the opportunity for social and occupational mobility. Programming and systems analysis are now standard parts of the curricula of most engineering schools, sometimes as part of electrical engineering, sometimes in separate departments. In

---

[10] As in any form of schooling, the ideological component is as important as the occupational in the training of programmers. At institutions like junior colleges, where the technical substance is so basic, the inculcation of acceptable employee attitudes looms as important as whatever software skills may be learned. An indication of how conscious managers are of this function of junior colleges comes from the remarks by a member of a recent panel on "Increasing the Productivity of the Programming Staff," sponsored by the American Management Association. The panelist, manager of edp operations and "technical systems" of a large textile and rug company, urged his fellow managers to look to two-year community and technical colleges for their coders and low-level programmers. Not only do the institutions provide some instruction in edp, he pointed out, they also provide a "general background, including that businesses are in business to make a profit."

Julian Pruitt, remarks before the session on "Increasing the Productivity of the Programming Staff," at "INFO '74," Americana Hotel, New York, New York, September 11, 1974.

contrast to junior colleges, they teach software courses which train the student to design and write programs rather than simply code them or operate the machines which run them.

Although it did not begin that way, since World War I engineering has become an avenue for individual advancement for working class men, if a short and early peaking one for those who don't change to another career before middle-age.[11] For many, it is the quickest, cheapest, and most easily accessible route from blue-collar to white-collar status.[12] The institutions which help them make the transition are, like the

---

[11] Modern engineering was one of the first occupations to offer interesting work, performed in a clean, well-lighted place, to sons of what used to be called the "working poor." After all, engineers got to wear white shirts and ties and were paid, if not as much as popularly imagined, better than most production occupations. For the hardworking individual, it was also easier to get started in engineering than in most other white-collar occupations. Schools were less fussy about family background and extensive training in classical languages than were the liberal arts schools. They tended to be much cheaper, too. Some even offered work-study programs that eased the financial burden further as well as giving the meritorious but socially unconnected young man access to potential employers. But the irony of the opportunity—and the end results— should not be overlooked. The rapid expansion of the engineering industries, the proliferation of relatively inexpensive training institutions, and even the relatively high salaries in the occupation, were possible only because the work of engineering was being made progressively routine and trivial on the level of the individual engineering worker. The engineer's work and production role, in other words, were being made to resemble conventional (blue-collar) production workers although the superficial trappings of "middle-class" position (see footnote following) such as dress remained. True, salaries were higher, but only at time of entry. The old saw that engineers start high and end low needs only the qualifier that they also peak early and find themselves under great pressure to leave after a decade. The young men who went into the field looking for occupational security absent in the blue-collar occupations found themselves in one of the most cyclical of all industries. Young graduates excited at being actively recruited at the beginning of a cyclical upturn found themselves being eased out at the end of the cycle (or at most, the end of a following cycle), and replaced with another crop of enthusiastic new graduates who would do essentially the same work for less money.

[12] "White-collar" and "status" are both fuzzy, misleading, not to say loaded terms, and to combine them compounds the deception several times over. Nowadays, white-collar means virtually nothing as an indicator of one's ability to control one's own life or the lives of others. It means almost as little in terms of the nature of a person's work and the income gotten from that work. The president of the Chase Manhatten Bank and the high school student who serves your hamburger and fries both wear ties. The Chairman of the Board of IBM, an installation manager of one of the company's branches, and a computer mechanic (euphemistically called "customer service representatives") all wear ties too. That proves nothing except that IBM is a company fond of ties on its male employees.

Status is a fancy Latin word which means place or standing. Most Americans right now are very confused about their standing and offering to place them on their collars amounts to a cruel joke.

White-collar, blue-collar, gray-collar, etc., are popular terms, however, and with the preceding objections kept in mind, I will use them when they promise to do a minimum of damage.

community colleges, often publicly funded and equally sensitive to the personnel requirements of potential employers. Ties between the institutions and employers are strong for more than reasons of mutual respect for the other's role. Engineering faculty are regularly employed as consultants by the same industries (including various government agencies) who hire their students. The practice is approved, often enthusiastically, by the engineering institutions. It is considered helpful in placing graduates and sounding out corporate and government underwriting of institutional projects, endowment, scholarships, and so on.

Engineering schools, unlike junior colleges, have more than just a local market for their products. Engineers receive more intensive training than do junior college-trained technicians. Their work is both more complex and requires more time-consuming and expensive instruction. It usually, but not always, commands higher pay. As a consequence, technicians have been given progressively more of the work formerly done by engineers, and they now outnumber engineers several times over. The engineering schools are thus fewer in number and they must serve regional rather than local employers. In the case of the most prestigious, their graduates are recruited on a national scale.

Research institutions and schools of management

The third and last category of software training institution is considerably different from the first two and turns out yet a different kind of software specialist. At first glance it may appear arbitrary to put in the same category two such dissimilar schools as research and management institutions. There are, of course, differences between highly trained computer scientists and executives and managers sophisticated in the ways of electronic data processing. In terms of their *social* roles in the edp workplace, however, they perform similar functions. Let us look at each in turn.

Research institutions. Research institutions are involved in state-of-the-art development and research—in all scientific and engineering fields, not just computing—and are usually but mistakenly lumped together with conventional engineering colleges. But to call the Massachusetts Institute of Technology (or the California Institute of Technology or Carnegie-Mellon University) another engineering school, however distinguished, makes as much sense as calling IBM a distinguished maker of office machines. MIT, Cal Tech, and a handful of others are not in the business of training engineers, no matter what their popular images. The MITs and Cal Techs engage in research helpful to the science-based industries (and the military, needless to say) and they do it on a level most other engineering schools simply cannot match. They train people who will give form and substance to the mass of engineering workers turned out by the conventional schools. They also train technically sophisticated specialists in a wide range of areas who become corporate managers or executives or entrepreneurs if they do not become high-level researchers in industrial, academic, or government laboratories. This aspect of the "elite" engineering schools is not widely appreciated, except among the science-based industries and some government bureaus, both of which generously underwrite their operation. Finally, they produce men (and a few women) who oversee the workplace activities of less extensively trained specialists. If, in the lesser engineering schools, private faculty consulting is tolerated or even actively encouraged, at these institutions it is a way of life, almost a requirement for continued employment. MIT, for example, is the largest single academic recipient of Department of Defense monies; its faculty and staff are routinely contracted out to perform a variety of corporate and government undertakings. For practical purposes, MIT and the other institutions in its league are research and policy-advising arms of the state and of corporate America (Smith).

Schools of management. In *social* terms, then, the research institutions must also be considered managerial institutions. Similarly, schools of management have been quick to make use of the new techniques and tools produced by the research institutions. Under these circumstances it should come as no surprise that instruction in software in the elite universities is increasingly focused in their schools of management. Perhaps the most appropriate example comes from MIT, where during the past few years the largest programming enrollments have not been in that institution's notable Department of Computer Science or equally notable Department of Electrical Engineering, but in the Alfred Sloan School of Management. Similarly, Harvard offers extensive programming courses (although not, of course, necessarily its most technically elaborate) through its Graduate School of Business Administration. Comparable situations are found at the other elite universities.

Management and business school graduates are not primarily technical specialists, although many of them are that too. They are first and above all managers with enough technical training to know what their technical employees are doing and therefore how to properly evaluate and control them. Perhaps this is the best indication of all that managers make use of engineers and engineer-type workers as extensions of their own roles. Edp is not merely a fast, economical way of processing large quantities of information. The flow of information may be either a means of rearranging the relations between people in an organization, a product that organization sells, or both. In either case, edp becomes a central concern of managers. If a product, its production must be managed and controlled like any other. If it is an organizational (i.e., control) device, then the "information function" is a basic tool for managers, either in extending their knowledge and control or for expanding the source of information on which they make their decisions.

*   *   *   *

Formal software training, in short, is almost entirely an industry matter. The form and substance of instruction, the selection of instructional staff, even the recruitment of students, are all closely monitored and sometimes directly supervised by the industries which employ most programmer specialists.

The extent of industry control can be gauged by the nature and composition of the occupational organizations that have been formed to promote and give direction to programmer training in the United States. The most inclusive is AFIPS, the American Federation of Information Processing Societies. Membership is through constituent societies, the largest of which, with about 30,000 members, is the Association for Computing Machinery.[13] ACM, as its name suggests, is concerned with data processing hardware, but its attentions have increasingly focused on personnel testing, recruitment, training, and evaluation. ACM has provided computer programmer training institutions with guidelines for curriculum development and course content. A similar function is provided by the

---

[13] At this writing ACM is starting a survey of its membership which would include for the first time a tabulation of its members' occupations. Of the respondents in my interview sample, the only software specialists who were members of ACM were academics or management-level employees in industry or government or entrepreneurial consultants, and sometimes all at once. None of the nonmanagement employees belonged (several in fact had not heard of the organization). This seems reasonable after attending a number of ACM meetings and meetings of ACM's "special interest groups" over a period of years. At these, the only nonmanagers in attendance, other than academics, were high-level technical specialists. The latter were employed to do research and development work (e.g., the creation of new languages or operating systems), not production or applications programming.

Institute for Computer Professionals, which, like AFIPS, is made up of constituent societies.[14]

None of these can claim—none do claim—significant membership among nonmanagement, nonacademy software employees. Neither, of course, does the Data Processing Management Association, with 25,000 members. Only the small (1,000 member) Association of Computer Programmers and Analysts, which acts much like a trade union while shunning the title, is made up of nonmanagement software workers. All told, membership in ACM, ASM, DPMA and the smaller societies does not exceed 75,000, and this figure undoubtedly would be smaller if it were possible to factor out multiple memberships. This is less than 25% of the cautious and now dated tabulations of the 1970 census. If we use the upper limit of the National Bureau of Standards' 1973 estimate, the figure represents less than 8% of the total software workforce. The ordinary coder or programmer—not to mention the machine operator or keypunch operator—is not seriously involved.[15]

This must be considered the most important feature of the formal organization of software training: by and for whom it is organized. Programmers cannot claim, as do physicians or plumbers, that they are trained by their future peers and colleagues. Like other engineering workers, their training is not in their own hands, passed on from master to apprentice. On the contrary: programmer training is in the hands of their future employers, directly in the case of company schools and in-house training, indirectly in the case of institutions which exist to service local, regional, or national employers.

Software training, in summary, is apportioned to different kinds of institutions which prepare people for different kinds of software occupations. Community colleges, engineering schools, science institutes, and schools of management train

---

[14] The constituent societies of the American Federation of Information Processing Societies include the American Institute of Aeronautics and Astronautics, the American Institute of Certified Public Accountants, the American Society for Information Science, The American Statistical Society, the Association for Computing Machinery, the Data Processing Managers Association, the Society for Industrial and Applied Mathematics, and a number of smaller organizations.

[15] The grunts of the programming world don't participate for many reasons, not the least of which is that they don't perceive industry groups serving any particular interests of theirs. For another, the largest group, ACM, doesn't engage in enthusiastic recruiting anywhere except in university campuses and among industrial and government managers. Many companies, like IBM, discourage employees except managers from belonging to noncompany organizations other than the most innocuous, e.g., church groups, little leagues. On the other hand, they often subsidize managers by paying membership and subscription fees, as well as convention expenses.

people to do different sorts of things. Students who pass
through junior colleges learn how to code and are not usually
prepared to become systems analysts or data processing managers. On the other hand, graduates of schools of management
are not generally prepared for careers as coders in applications
programming. There is, in other words, an institutional division of labor between schools with respect to the kind of
software worker they produce.

But if programmer-training institutions differ in the kind of
student they produce, it must be noted that they are also likely
to differ in the kind of student who attends them. There are, as
far as I know, no hard and fast data to confirm this beyond
doubt, but two different sorts of information, one dealing with
software workers, the other with American education, suggest
that the social divisions of the larger American society are
reflected in the way students of different social backgrounds
are distributed among educational institutions.

The first is fragmentary and cannot be said to constitute an
objective portrait of the software workforce. As part of the
research conducted for this study, I interviewed nearly 100
software workers at all technical and bureaucratic levels, from
coders to data processing executives to software consultants to
high-level technical specialists. The group could not, let me
stress, be considered a random sample of programmers. The
interviews were gathered in a rolling stone manner: people
whom I interviewed suggested others for me to talk with, and
some of these in turn recommended still others. It was made up
almost entirely of easterners or people from the Midwest. It did
not reflect what is probably the national distribution of
software workers, since there were few employees of financial
or government organizations. Almost certainly there were
proportionately more analysts, high-level technical specialists,
and managers than in the software workforce as a whole.
About half were women.

This cannot, in any sense, constitute a portrait of American
programmers. Still, the group was characterized by a number
of attributes which, if at all similar to the programming population as a whole, indicates a clear pattern. For example, the
parents of coders and low-level applications programmers were
of modest economic and educational backgrounds. They were
typically high school graduates and worked as blue-collar or
clerical employees. A few owned, or had owned, marginal
small businesses—"mom and pop" stores, roofing and siding
businesses, and similar undertakings. The mothers were almost as well-educated as the fathers, but as a group they did
not work with their husbands in the wage labor workforce.

The situation of analysts, managers, and high-level programmers was very different. Their fathers counted among their ranks professionals of various sorts (physicians, lawyers, research scientists, etc.). The mothers were nearly as well-educated as their husbands, and more frequently than the mothers of coders and low-level programmers, they were employed outside the home.

The parental backgrounds of this very special group of software workers cannot establish any definite relationships for software workers as a whole. Although these can only be suggestive, there is considerably more certainty about the structure of the larger education system of which software training is a part. If software students in the various educational institutions do in fact come from significantly different social backgrounds, it would only reflect the organization of American education as a whole. Affluent and better educated families are more likely to send their children to college than are families of more modest means and education. When they do, they are also more likely to send them to the so-called elite schools. This does not mean, of course, that only members of elite families go to elite schools or that only the less affluent go to nonelite schools. It does mean that the rich are *more* likely to send their children to the best schools—or at any rate, the most expensive and prestigious—than are the nonrich, while the latter are more likely to send their children to the worst schools—or no school at all. It is not very important, by the way, that there are many exceptions to the general pattern. It is only important that *as a rule* American education channels people from particular social backgrounds into particular kinds of work.

It isn't hard to illustrate how the channeling process works in practice. Elite schools, like Harvard, MIT, Stanford, and Cal Tech, turn out proportionately more professionals (doctors, lawyers, scientists, academics), as well as managers, businessmen, and other high-prestige, high-income people than do local community colleges. Engineering colleges, of course, turn out more certified engineers than either. It might be objected that this is the proverbial exercise in comparing apples and oranges. This is precisely the point. Liberal arts colleges, community colleges, engineering schools, and science universities exist to train different people to do different things. But because the schools also differ according to the social class origins of the students who attend them, the schools play an important role in reinforcing social divisions as well. It really doesn't matter for our purposes why this is so or whether it should be so. It is only necessary to understand that, for whatever reasons, the structure of American education as a whole is divided into clear-cut categories defined by the social class backgrounds of their students.[16] The social class differences of the larger society, reinforced and given an occupational content by the educational system, are then reproduced in the social relations of the workplace (Bowles and Gintis, pp. 203–223).

With respect to software training, it is possible to discern the emergence of a similar social division, one which channels the sons and daughters of the less affluent into low-level technical and clerical positions, while directing the children of the comparatively more prosperous to positions in the field which offer considerably more in the way of interesting work, material rewards, career opportunities, and high social standing.

If this is indeed the beginning of a trend, it should not come as a surprise. The software occupations have been, in a remarkably short time, thoroughly restructured to resemble other technical and engineering occupations. Similarly, institutions which provide formal training to software workers at all levels have also been organized to resemble the training institutions of conventional engineering occupations. Is it not likely, then, that they will also come to resemble both in their social divisions?

[16] The differences in student background and career lines are often the differences between very expensive private colleges—astronomically out of reach for most American families—and the less expensive state institutions. This is particularly true in the Northeast, which has a long tradition of elite private colleges as well as a well-defined network of private (and equally expensive) preparatory schools which supply them with upper-class applicants. On the other hand, even within a state system there is usually a difference between the nature and often the cost of the institutions and the class of origin of the people who attend them. Thus, California's elaborate college system was carefully organized into three major levels. The first was made up of a small number of traditional liberal arts colleges, with affiliated professional and graduate schools of national rank. Admission to these elite colleges—Berkeley, UCLA, Santa Barbara, etc.—was restricted to applicants with the highest grades, best test scores, most glowing recommendations, and other evidence of high academic accomplishments. A second level was made up of a larger group of undergraduate colleges, usually not affiliated with graduate or professional schools (other than schools of education). Very often they began as state teacher training institutions and during the 1950s had their scope broadened a bit to include a wider liberal arts curriculum. Admission standards at these schools are less stringent than the first group's. The third and final level is made up of "junior" colleges—two-year institutions which offer training in explicitly vocational areas, ranging from clerical skills to drafting to bookkeeping and accountancy. Admission to these schools is open to anyone with a degree from an accredited high school.

A study of the students in the California system showed precisely the same distribution pattern within the state system as we have been discussing for the American system as a whole. The elite liberal arts colleges had a higher percentage of students from affluent, better-educated homes than did the schools in the second tier, while the latter had a higher percentage than the junior colleges (Clark). I have singled out the California experience because it has been used as a model for other states, including New York, which vies with it for having the largest system of state supported higher education. See also Smith, Ch. 1.

References   American Federation of Information Processing Societies (1972). *Proceedings 1972 Spring Joint Computer Conf.* Montvale, N.J.: AFIPS Press.

Bowles, Samuel, and Herbert Gintis (1976). *Schooling in Capitalist America.* New York: Basic Books.

Clark, Burton (1960). *The Open Door College: A Case Study.* New York: McGraw-Hill.

Goldstine, Herman (1972). *The Computer: From Pascal to Von Neumann.* Princeton: Princeton University Press.

Gilchrist, Bruce, and Richard E. Weber (1972a). Sources of trained computer personnel—a quantitative survey. *Proceedings 1972 Spring Joint Computer Conf.* Montvale, N.J.: AFIPS Press.

Gilchrist, Bruce, and Richard E. Weber (1972b). Employment of trained computer personnel—a quantitative survey. *Proceedings 1972 Spring Joint Computer Conf.* Montvale, N.J.: AFIPS Press.

Hamblen, John W. (1972). Production and Utilization of Computer Manpower in the U.S. *Proceedings 1972 Spring Joint Computer Conf.* Montvale, N.J.: AFIPS Press.

Hoos, Ida (1974). *Systems Analysis in Public Policy: A Critique.* Berkeley and Los Angeles: University of California Press.

Layton, Edwin (1969). Science, business, and American engineers. In Perrucci and Gerstl.

Noble, David (1977). *America by Design: Science, Technology and the Rise of Corporate Capitalism.* New York: Knopf.

Perrucci, Robert, and Joel Gerstl (1969). *The Engineer and the Social System.* New York: John Wiley & Sons.

Smith, David N. (1974). *Who Rules the Universities? An Essay in Class Analysis.* New York and London: Monthly Review Press.

3 De-skilling and fragmentation

Introduction If programming has experienced a separation of head and hand work, it has only followed the pattern of most other industrial occupations. Almost all modern workplaces divide work and separate people. They impose narrow limits on personal involvement in the work process. They restrict workers to anonymous fragments of larger undertakings which for the most part they neither control nor understand. Perhaps because large and impersonal forms of organization have become so common, it is easy to forget that they are human, not natural, inventions. Workplaces do not, after all, organize themselves. Conveyor belts do not turn themselves on. Edp machines do not invent their own operating systems. People—at least some of them—do all of these things. They also decide if a workplace will be large or small, integrated or fragmented, organized hierarchically or along democratic lines. They do so, moreover, in a very special context. If the maker of a product—canned tomatoes, automated billing systems, neckties—wants to make a profit, he must sell his product for more than it costs to make it. The key to profitmaking is to reduce costs, and in this society the major way of reducing costs is to reduce the cost of labor. In economic terms, this is often called ''increasing productivity.'' In practice, it means making more of a product with fewer skilled, and therefore fewer expensive, workers. The task is accomplished in a manner by now so commonplace that we take it, too, for granted: turning out huge quantities of a standardized product, whether automobiles, hamburgers, utility bills, newspapers, prestuffed turkeys—the list is endless. Labor costs can be reduced because the work necessary to turn out a standardized product can itself be standardized. This is what I mean by de-skilling. It is a deliberate effort to transform work made up of separate but interdependent tasks into a larger number of simpler, routine, and unrelated tasks. Such routinized subtasks can then be parcelled out to workers who do only one, or at most a few, of them over and over, and nothing else. Such workers, obviously, need less skill than the workers who performed all the tasks of the more complex original work.

All modern industrial workplaces are organized on this principle. Its chief symbol has been the assembly line, made famous, though not invented, by Henry Ford. But the routinization and fragmentation of work can and does exist without the physical presence of an assembly line. With or without a conveyor belt, the principle is the same. All that is needed is (1) an unvarying good or service and (2) an unvarying way of turning it out. Today, mass production techniques and their attendant use of unskilled and semi-skilled mass-production workers have been applied everywhere, from billing departments to fast food restaurants to the care and feeding of hospital patients, as well as to other workplaces where the assembly line, in the literal sense, has never been known.

The result has been an apparent paradox. We live in a society which depends on the most complex and sophisticated technology in the world. Yet the majority of people who work in this society possess only the most rudimentary work skills.[1] The paradox does not represent a contradiction. On the contrary: it is cause and effect. People have experienced a process of de-skilling because the new technology has made mass-production techniques feasible for more and more workplaces and therefore has reduced the need for human skills at the point of production. In effect, the skills and talents of a relatively tiny proportion of the labor force—research scientists, production engineers, systems analysts, and similar creative workers—have been used to make "unproductive" the skills of a vast majority of the rest.

The de-skiller de-skilled

The de-skilling process has been accelerated with the widespread application of electronic data processing. Computer-controlled machinery are now vital parts of the national work flow, e.g., accounting and inventory control in commercial

[1] This should not be a startling discovery, although apparently it has been for some. See the study done for the Secretary of Health, Education and Welfare, published as *Work in America*. Less surprised analyses of the trend are found in Braverman (especially the chapters on "Clerical Workers" and "Scientific Management") and Marglin. Marglin's paper had been widely circulated before publication and has been a major factor in drawing the attention of many of his fellow economists to the study of workplace relations.

settings, numerical control in manufacture, and so on. Computers have allowed managers to replace secretaries with clerical workers, while clerical workers have been reduced to keypunch operators. In the same way, machinists have been demoted to machine tenders, cooks turned into servers of micro-wave oven-heated hotdogs, etc.[2]

In spite of its complexity, edp hardware shares an important feature with the more conventional conveyor belt: it does nothing by itself until someone tells it what to do. Given this, it seems reasonable to expect that the people who tell computers what to do—programmers—would have jobs which are considerably more skilled, more responsible, and more creative than the work done by most other Americans.

Yet, I contended in Chapter 1 that the people who guide the computer's operations are, like other workers, becoming less and less skilled. (I should say at the outset that the *most* skilled software specialists are today without doubt more skilled than their predecessors; the de-skilling trend refers to the *average* level of programmer skill.) In this chapter I will examine how and why the process of de-skilling has come about.

To begin with, the movement to lower average skills among software workers is regularly commented on by software and data processing managers. Just as regularly, certain explanations are offered. The most common is that edp has grown so quickly and the hardware and programming techniques have been developed, put into service, modified, and replaced at such dizzying speed, that the software field out of necessity has had to use an expanding proportion of relatively young and inexperienced workers. A typical assessment comes from F. T. Baker of the International Business Machine Corporation:

> Production programming projects today are often staffed by relatively junior programmers with at most a few years of experience. This condition is primarily the result of the rapid development of the computer and the burgeoning of its applications. (Baker, 1972a, p. 56)

The explanation is ingenuous and self-serving. Hardware and software techniques have come and gone so quickly precisely because hardware makers, software "vendors," and edp users have wanted to use computers without having to also use highly skilled and very expensive software experts. De-skilling has come about because of efforts by the industry to reduce labor costs in order to expand the use of edp machines and

---

[2] The most compelling description of the process is found in Braverman. A look into the future—made with eerie accuracy in 1952—is in Kurt Vonnegut's novel, *Player Piano*.

techniques, not the other way around. For example, software managers routinely get rid of older, more experienced programmers and replace them with younger, less experienced programmers. The reasons are straightforward: it costs less to employ a young programmer than an older one who has accumulated not only lots of pay increments, but lots of fringe benefits and lots of pension rights as well. Managers are quite open about the procedure. A concise explanation was provided by a project manager during an interview about her work and her job:

> If a programmer has been with [her company] more than six or seven years, he's probably earning $15–16k [i.e., thousand] per year. A programmer right out of school can do the same thing after five or six months for 10k. It's all a bottom-line consideration.[3]

Easing out older, more expensive workers is not an invention of the computing world. Software managers are only making use of an established process which has been around so long it has become virtually an adjunct to the business cycle, particularly in the case of traditional engineering workers (Fischer and Lesser).

But managers could not replace more experienced and more skilled employees with less experienced and less skilled employees unless the latter are able to do the work. The fragmentation of programming into suboccupations like coding, program design, and systems analysis suggests that the industry has been able to introduce changes in the way programming is done to render it less complex and more routine. Of all the changes, three are central:

(1) the extensive use of pre-packaged or "canned" programs
(2) changes in the way programming work itself is performed, especially the widespread use of "structured programming" and its derivations
(3) changes in the way programming work is organized, notably the use of the "Chief Programmer Team"

Canned programs

Canned programs are pre-packaged applications programs for data processing jobs which, while not identical, are similar in

---

[3] It is of added interest that this particular "shop" did not engage in the routine, bookkeeping operations focused on in this chapter. The company produced advanced minicomputers and their operating (software) systems. It suggests that even in complex software work many of the tasks can be performed by relatively unskilled programmers. The manager herself, it is interesting to note, was only 28 at the time of the interview.

their basic features, e.g., payroll calculations, inventory control, or other repetitive, bookkeeping operations. They are essentially extensions of the stored program principle. In effect, the use of canned programs represents a joint decision by software sellers and software buyers to make the problems fit the solutions at hand.

For the purchaser or client there are several advantages. It means being able to buy or rent a ready-made program which is, he hopes, a tested and proved product, without the bother and expense of employing highly skilled software experts to design, write, test, modify, maintain, and update an *ad hoc* solution to a unique problem. Since the product has been in a sense mass-produced, while limited, it is also likely to be cheaper than writing and installing a one-of-a-kind program. The ready availability of a high volume, relatively cheap product also means that smaller organizations which could not afford any kind of in-house or internal data processing can now buy all sorts of edp services by contracting for a complete "package" of software as well as hardware.

For the software seller, the advantages are if anything even greater. In addition to expanding the market for his product, the vendor is in a position to lower his labor costs in precisely the ways just described. Relatively few "super programmers" are needed to write programs in comparison to the total number of data processing workers of all kinds who run them. If the programs are well-designed and well-written to begin with [see pp. 56–61 below on structured programming], a less skilled programmer can perform most of the modifications necessary to adapt an existing program to the needs of several different clients. In fact, programs constructed with enough care can in certain applications be left entirely to machine operators who have been trained to adapt packages from one client's requirements to another's. Programmers become necessary only for trouble shooting or for unexpected, major modifications.

Canned programs were early, relatively simple devices for routinizing much software work and thus creating a whole new and less expensive suboccupation of the semi-skilled "applications programmer." But their use represented a social arrangement for the most part, rather than a technical breakthrough. They failed to provide a solution to the problem that vexed managers most: how to simplify the software itself. In a sense, canned programs limited the standardization of programs to their consumption rather than their production. They still had to be written in the same slow, artisan-like way as any other. In effect, managers and edp users who had available to them in the early 1960s powerful and sophisticated hardware found themselves in almost the same position as the users of the early plug-board computers. The machines worked below their capacity because programmers produced programs slowly, and when finished, spent much of their time correcting errors.

Structured programming

All this changed in the early 1960s with the introduction of an entirely new way of organizing and coding programs. Structured programming was nothing less than a radical break with programming's short but universal tradition of idiosyncratic software production. Even after the analyst's emergence in the 1950s as the conceptual architect and organizer of a programming project, programming remained very much an individual affair. Programs, including the largest and most complex systems, were usually put together from start to finish by the same individual or group that worked on every aspect of the job: definition of the edp problem, organization and method of data entry, program logic, processing, and even application. Testing, debugging (i.e., finding and correcting program or design errors), modification, maintenance, and the rest of the tasks associated with keeping a program in working condition were also the responsibilities of the same person or group.

Programmers (and analysts) followed a logic and procedures which were largely of their own making. Their decision to use a given instruction or sequence of instructions was determined by a combination of individual training, experience, skill, and imagination. Programs made in this manner had distinct "personalities" which reflected their creators. Some were terse and elegant. Others were long and highly detailed. Some programmers, because of their experience with particular languages or operating systems or even the hardware, could make the machine "do tricks" which were mysteries to the uninitiated.

Among the uninitiated were many managers and users. And this made for some tension. In general, the creativity of individual workers made software managers dependent on individual programmers for the well-being of any given program. Some programmers developed extraordinary skills in one type of software problem or in a particular language or in keeping a program operational once put into service. To a large extent, programmers, not their managers or even their colleagues, exercised final control over software production: only the writer of a given program could guarantee that a program would work the way it was supposed to. Programmers, in short, had a form of job security as long as their programs were being used. Managers and owners in these circumstances are vulnerable to all sorts of calamities. Programmers can fall off mountains and die. They can quit and go to work for a competitor. Or, they could simply demand more money or changes in working conditions—and get them because of their indispensability. Disgruntled programmers could even sabotage their own work—and feel confident that no one could fix it.

If none of these profit-robbing things happened, from the perspective of managers the production of software by idiosyncratic methods posed still other, equally serious problems. Managers believe that the most time-consuming and therefore the most expensive part of software production is finding out why the program someone has just written doesn't work and then fixing it. This makes their dependence on programmers a double one. Their products are made by highly skilled, expensive workers whose time is spent fixing programs instead of turning out finished products which could be quickly made and quickly used or sold.

To make the production of programs independent of individual programmers—in much the same way cars are produced independently of individual automobile workers—various schemes had been proposed from time to time to standardize what programmers did. Generally, these were without lasting impact. They were the software equivalent of helpful hints to the homemaker, focusing on specific coding problems, organizational structures, personnel techniques, and so on. Unlike such piecemeal approaches, structured programming offered an entirely new way of writing programs, elegant in theory and unambiguous in principle. Indeed, the principle was simple: if managers could not yet have machines which wrote programs, at least they could have programmers who worked like machines. Until human programmers were eliminated altogether, their work would be made as machine-like—that is, as simple and limited and routine—as possible. Briefly, programmers using structured programming would be limited to a handful of logical procedures which they could use—no others were permitted. They could call only for certain kinds of information; they could ask only specified questions about that information; on the basis of the answer they received to their question, they could call for a particular machine operation (or an answer to another, approved question); when the operation was completed, they had to stop. No deviation from this logical sequence is allowed. They could not, for example, call for information not contained in the original data set assigned to them. They could not call for a machine operation not among those approved for their particular task. [A fuller discussion of the logic of structured programming appears in the Appendix.]

Obviously, the programmer's ability to make decisions about his program, if using structured programming techniques, has been considerably reduced. But this is not all. The scope of the task that can be undertaken has also been considerably reduced. At the basic level of coding, elaborate, complex logical manipulations are virtually impossible, given the limitations on what the programmer may do. This is not to say that it is no longer possible to construct elaborate and complex software systems at all. It means instead that such complex structures will be made up of more, smaller, simpler manipulations instead of fewer, complex ones, somewhat in the manner of making three right turns in order to make one left turn. The distinction is basic: in this way the ability to produce large and complex systems has not been impared, *only the opportunity* of the average programmer to produce them.

For managers, the advantages of this sort of programming are enormous. If there are only a few pre-determined ways of ordering a program's logic, considerably less skill, training, and experience are required to grasp the major logical tools of the trade. Moreover, since the procedures are few, universal, and well-understood, one programming routine will develop much like all others. Mistakes are no longer idiosyncratic but systemic; they can be found and corrected, therefore, systematically by anyone who has mastered the relatively simple rules of program organization and coding. Both writing and debugging are further facilitated by structured programming's logical partner, modularization, which breaks down an entire software system into limited-function, discrete units, written independently and then fitted together in a pre-determined way to form a single system. "Modules" can be individually checked for errors while the rest of the system functions at a reduced level. This is in contrast to the situation typical of conventional programs which could be brought down completely by just one elusive "bug."

Structured programming and modularization thus achieved two long cherished managerial goals at once. They freed managers from dependence on individual high-level software workers. They also made possible for the first time a genuine job-based fragmentation of labor in programming. Until structured programming, the common industry-wide divisions between analyst, programmer, and coder could be no more than arbitrary divisions of authority and control. Actual work tasks inevitably overlapped at all levels. Structured programming, on the other hand, reorganized not only the formal relations of the workplace but the content of the work itself. A hierarchy of authority could now be established by arranging various job fragments in a rank-order on the basis of either skill or an understanding of the task as a whole or both. *Managers* defined edp problems and gave them to high-level *analysts* or similar specialists to design the software system. Each component was given to a separate *project group* (which might have only a single programmer/coder if the task was simple enough) which worked independently of the others. In complex systems, each module could be so narrowly defined that they were essentially coding exercises, making no sense to the people who did the work. The completed tasks or modules were then sent back to the analysts to be combined and tested as a system. The assembled final product could then be turned over to the client for use.[4]

Structured programming, in short, has become the software manager's answer to the assembly line, minus the conveyor belt but with all the other essential features of a mass-production workplace: a standardized product made in a standardized way by people who do the same limited tasks over and over without knowing how they fit into a larger undertaking.[5]

Chief programmer teams

After the development of structured programming, all that managers needed in their quest for mass-produced software was an organizational form around which to arrange the newly created fragments of programming work. The Chief Programmer Team (CPT) was soon created to fill the need. The CPT is little more than a formalization of the way programmer groups tend to be organized in practice when structured programming techniques are used. According to one of its most influential proponents, F. T. Baker, the Chief Programmer Team

[4] The classic early statement of the principles of structured programming— invariably cited in subsequent articles, texts, instruction manuals, etc.—is given by Dijkstra (1968; 1972). But see also Introduction, pp. 9–10.

[5] I showed preliminary drafts of this discussion to several programmers for their comment. One response, from a high-level specialist employed in an engineering workplace, was especially relevant. Structured programming, modularization, and their variations, he pointed out, were useful tools in the hands of highly skilled people. They are, after all, simply formalizations of logical methods which had always been employed, although haphazardly and without much system, from programming's early days. The *organizational* importance of structured programming is in its *social application;* that is, it has generally been adopted by managers in large workplaces not to facilitate good programming, but to make it easier to manage programmers.

is organized around a nucleus of a Chief Programmer, a Backup Programmer and a Programming Librarian. The Chief Programmer is both the prime architect and the key coder of the system. The Backup Programmer works closely with the Chief to design and produce the system's key elements, as well as providing essential insurance that development can continue should the Chief leave the project. . . . This Team nucleus, usually assisted by a systems analyst, designs and begins development of the system. The Team is then augmented by additional programmers who produce the remainder of the code under the close supervision of the Chief and Backup Programmers. (Baker, 1972b, pp. 339–340)

Baker adds another organizational comment:

In addition to the functional organization . . . the Team operates in a highly disciplined fashion using principles of structured programming. . . . These couple a top-down evolutionary approach to systems development with the application of formal rules governing control flow within modules. . . .

Application of these rules permits a program to be read from beginning to end with no control jumps. It therefore simplifies testing and greatly enhances visibility and understandability of programs. (p. 340)

It is all here, quite plain and quite explicit: the major division between conceptual and routine tasks; a ''Backup Programmer'' who acts as both apprentice and potential replacement for the chief creative (and supervisory) worker; the modularization, i.e., fragmentation and standardization of work into routine segments.

All that is missing is a final legitimizing touch, and even this is provided:

[The CPT is] a functional programming organization similar in concept to a surgical team. Members of the team are specialists who assist the Chief Programmer in developing a program system, much as nurses, anesthesiologists and laboratory personnel assist a surgeon in performing an operation. (p. 339)

It is not important how accurate the analogy is. By accident or design, Baker (and lots of others, since the surgical analogy is highly popular among managers) has selected a workplace whose organization is the most structured, hierarchicalized, and status-bound of any in the industrial world. Whether, too, by accident or design, the analogy captures some of the subtleties of the real division of labor, as well as the divisions of status and authority and control. If the real division of the work tasks between surgeon, assistant, other attending physicians, nurses, *et al.* are vague and overlapping, the social and political divisions are not, nor are the rewards.

Structured programming techniques and Chief Programmer Teams are not yet found in every programming workplace. In part this is the result of the different labor and bureaucratic needs of organizations. Small software firms (or organizations which maintain small software departments) are by virtue of both their size and the multiple demands put on their software employees less in need of the workplace relationships structured programming and CPTs provide. On the other hand, CPTs are being rapidly introduced in large organizations, probably because these are the places which most need to insert software workers into their bureaucratized structures. Because they are so large, they are also highly visible and influential in the rest of the industry and thus act as models.

Programming as mass production work

Canned programs, structured programming, and modularization are designed to make the supervision of software workers by managers easier and more like the supervision of other workers, i.e., by restructuring the work so that simply by doing it the worker regulates himself. The organization of the work and workplace are thereby turned against the worker; regulation and supervision become, for all material purposes, automatic. Such managerial techniques have made possible the use of relatively less skilled programmers for what were formerly the most complex software tasks. It was in a similar way that the standardization of auto-making allowed auto manufacturers to replace mechanics and carriage builders with an alliance (although, to be sure, a hostile one) of automotive engineers and semi-skilled assembly-line workers.

To date, programmers have not been reduced to quite the same level of fragmented activity as autoworkers. Even coding has not become the equivalent of putting the same nut on the same bolt on the same wheel, car after car. But the social and individual consequences have been remarkably similar. For example, "modules" can be so reduced in size and function that people who work on similar ones often have no idea of what people who work on slightly different modules are doing. In large systems, the differences may be unbreachable. In an interview with a coder working on systems software for a new computer, the following exchange took place:

Q. When do you go for lunch?
A. 11:42.
Q. Exactly?
A. Right.
Q. Who goes with you?
A. A girlfriend of mine . . . [she] was in my [in-house] programming class.

Q. What do you speak about?

A. People, friends. . . .

Q. You don't talk about programming or things that happen at work?

A. Only if we have complaints . . . it's been a rough day, things like that. Our work things are too different. I wouldn't understand her work and she wouldn't understand mine.

Q. Why? Are your work tasks so different?

A. I do maintenance—like records and readings—and I work in PL/I, mostly. She works in assembler—her programming is in machines. It's completely different.

The two women—both recently out of high school—had been put through the same in-house training program only a few months before.

But programming is not the same as assembly line work, at least not yet. Programming, even coding, is still primarily a mind-skill and there are few hard and fast rules of behavior which managers can compare against an efficiency expert's model in order to check performance.[6] Similarly, most managers, even those who were trained as analysts or programmers, aren't always capable of judging when a program is written well or badly. In most cases, they have to take what programmers offer and wait to see if it works.

Programmers thus persist in being something of an anomaly in the modern workplace: they are employees, but they are in a position to control much of how they will go about doing their programs—the final product—and to some extent even the form the final product will take. Even the careful use of structured programming methods does not for the present give managers absolute control over all aspects of software production.

An occupation which remains so resistant to precise definition and therefore resistant to easy fragmentation and quick standardization is in an unusually good position to defend its members from outside control, including managerial control. Workplace autonomy of this kind threatens the whole carefully contrived balance of hierarchical relations and thus of managerial authority. Managers have responded to the threat with a variety of strategies. We have already seen that one strategy involves getting rid of programmers wherever possible by "wiring in" more and more software in "smart machines." Others—such as encouraging internal regulation *via* a profes-

---

[6] This is not to say that managers have not tried. A common technique is to use the machine as overseer, by having it note machine time used to run whole programs or modules, keep tabulations of the number of program instructions per module (one widely used approach limits the total to 11 or 12), and perform other such bookkeeping functions which lend themselves to comparison against (management-set) standards.

sional ideology, fabricating the so-called "dual ladder" structures used in other technical workplaces, and the shaping of employee attitudes and career expectations—will be discussed in later chapters. In the following chapter, we examine how managers have structured the everyday work relations to establish and reinforce their control of the software workplace.

References   Baker, F. T. (1972a). Chief programmer team management of production programming. *IBM Systems* 1:56–73.

Baker, F. T. (1972b). System quality through structured programming. *Proceedings 1972 Fall Joint Computer Conf.* Montvale, New Jersey: AFIPS Press (pp. 339–343).

Braverman, Harry (1974). *Labor and Monopoly Capital: The Degradation of Labor in the Twentieth Century.* New York and London: Monthly Review Press.

Dahl, Ole Johan, Edsger Dijkstra, and C. A. R. Hoare (1972). *Structured Programming.* London and New York: Academic Press.

Dijkstra, Edsger W. (1968). Go-to statement considered harmful. *Comm. ACM* XI, 3:147–148.

Dijkstra, Edsger W. (1972). Notes on Structured Programming, in Dahl, Dijkstra, and Hoare.

Fischer, Britta, and Mary Lesser (1973). Engineers. *Science for the People* V, 3:16–21.

Marglin, Stephen (1974). What Do Bosses Do? The Origins and Functions of Hierarchy in Capitalist Production. *Rev. Rad. Pol. Econ.* VI, 2:60–112.

United States Department of Health, Education and Welfare (1973). *Work in America.* Cambridge: MIT Press.

Vonnegut, Kurt, Jr. (1952). *Player Piano.* New York: Delacorte Press.

4

The programmer's workplace: Part I the "shop"

Introduction It was not so long ago that programmers were made out to be a tribe of magicians who performed mysteries hidden from the understanding of ordinary human beings. The "typical" programmer was an unkempt eccentric, part wizard, part misanthrope, who preferred the company of electronic brains to human ones. Bleary-eyed, usually bearded, he dwelled in a forbidden place called a "cubicle"—preferably adjacent to the computer—furnished only with paper, pencil, and army cot. He worked, like true magicians, mostly at night, making only occasional daylight visits to claim payment for services rendered.

Perhaps some programmers conformed to the stereotype; perhaps, even now, some still do. Any new and uncertain undertaking, after all, will attract the marginal loner, the fanatic possessed of and possessed by a single-minded vision, while the contented—or the less dedicated—will hold back to await developments.

But most such programmer-as-misanthrope talk was and is pure fancy, the product of self-serving imaginations of managers frustrated by their initial inability to handle these new employees. Before structured programming, and especially before the role of the systems analyst was formalized, programming had resisted easy integration into the bureaucracies of most organizations. It is not hard to see why. In a bureaucracy, each person is assigned a specific place according to the role or task he or she performs. In theory, each role or task is carefully and precisely defined to set it apart from others. Each is associated with clearly specified degrees of autonomy, power, and authority, as well as different rewards, responsibilities, and opportunities. Finally, the various tasks and roles which compose the bureaucracy also constitute a *hierarchy*. Hierarchies are social versions of a ladder, because each task or role is a rung or step which leads to the next in a regular, predictable way. The hierarchy, again in theory, allows an individual on a given step to move as far up the bureaucratic ladder as his or her talents and ambition will allow.

Software work, like other mind-work, does not readily lend itself to this sort of narrow definition of work and tidy division of people into discrete "job descriptions." Even today, categories as broad and poorly defined as coder, programmer, and analyst are largely arbitrary and routinely crossed in the practice of writing a program. They are social divisions, as between manager and managed, more than technical divisions of labor, and yield when the realities of the production process demand cooperative effort.

The difficulty managers encountered and still encounter in their attempts to incorporate programmers into traditional hierarchies has encouraged the creation of a mythology about the character and workplace behavior of the people who make the computer work. If you take managers at their word, programming remains an undertaking always on the verge of chaos. It is populated by either undisciplined anarchists or sullen slackers—or both. Programmers are by their nature (and this is a moral comment as well as a psychological evaluation) narrow-minded specialists whose major interests are esoteric games ("programming for the computer instead of the client") and whose primary occupational goals are jobs with regular pay increments and no responsibilities. It goes without saying that order is brought to all this potential chaos only through the great effort of managers who, unlike their charges, are "generalists" with a clear view of the "Big Picture," the end to which the work of the programmer will be put.

In reality, persistant industry efforts to routinize and de-skill software work, particularly in the use of structured programming and its offshoots, have taken a severe and probably a fatal toll on programming's population of eccentrics. Nowadays, programmers look like most other white-collar industrial workers. It would be hard, for example, to pick a programmer out of a group of electrical engineers or technicians; the fellow in the beard and sandals is probably from public relations or a psychologist from the personnel department. Programmers, to put it plainly, look like white-collar industrial employees— engineers, technicians, clerks—because their work and workplaces have been carefully shaped to look as much as possible like these conventional occupations and their workplaces. Programming's integration into conventional bureaucracies is now well advanced, in other words, thanks largely to the efforts of managers to arrange and control the relations of the software workplace. This is not a conspiracy or secret concealed from the rest of the world by devious software managers. They are simply—and quite explicitly—acting like managers are supposed to, manipulating people and controlling things in order to control work and worker. The place to examine how they have done so is the software workplace itself.

The social structure of the programming workplace

In Chapter 5 we will look at the issues of pay, promotion, and careers for software workers. Here we will concentrate on the everyday relations created by the social structure of the software workplace. By social structure I mean the regular, established relations of power and influence between different kinds of people. The relations may be formal and officially sanctioned (as in the prerogatives of managers to evaluate employees) or informal and illicit (as in the decision of employees to work at an unusually slow or inefficient manner in order to discredit an unpopular manager or policy). It includes but is not limited to the ability to influence the fate of others in such matters as pay, promotion, and even employment itself. It also includes such hard to measure things as getting along with managers or employees or working in a tense or congenial environment.

The analysis of software workplace relations presented here has been derived from several sources. The most important has been direct observation of three software workplaces: a systems programming group in a large computer manufacturing company;[1] an applications group in another manufacturing facility, part of a diversified industrial conglomerate; and the computer center of a large university. Formal interviews and informal discussions with programmers, analysts, managers, consultants, and academics provided additional valuable information. Finally, four published sources were especially use-

---

[1] In case there are any impulses to second-guess the identity of the computer manufacturing workplace, let me make the following disclaimer. Although I live near IBM's Endicott, New York computer production plant, this was *not* the computer manufacturing workplace I observed, nor was any other IBM facility. I did interview a number of IBMers (and a number of ex-IBMers), but not where they worked. Those familiar with the company will not be surprised that an outsider was not given free run of the premises.

ful: Weinberg, Pettigrew, Hebden, and Greenbaum. The shortcomings of Weinberg's book have already been noted; it remains, however, invaluable and provocative. Hebden and Pettigrew (although the latter's data are now 10 and 19 years old) document the process of the separation of "clerical" from "analytical" work and the parallel social divisions emerging between coders and analysts in England. Greenbaum's paper is an analytically precise and insightful memoir of a former programmer and IBMer turned edp instructor.[2]

Physical setting

If some early programmers lived the life of recluses, present-day programmers do precisely the opposite. Programmers today work in highly organized settings. They have managers. Their managers have managers. *Their* managers report to section heads or division vice-presidents. Except when done in a few "software laboratories," programming is hardly ever an isolated, self-contained activity. The result of a programmer's work is a product which is either sold to a client (whether external or in-house), used as a management tool, or employed as technical adjunct to a production process. Programming, in other words, is only one kind of work among many and programmers are in regular and in some cases constant contact with nonprogrammers as well as with fellow software specialists.

Because they work in organizations which are not primarily software workplaces, programmers have been forced to adapt their work habits and their workplace relations to the demands imposed on them by the parent organization. The most general of these "adjustments" have already been discussed: the attempt to divide "hand" work from "head" work; efforts to progressively reduce the tasks of programming into their smallest possible parts; and the parcelling out of these fragments to different people (coders, programmers, analysts, managers) who occupy different "rungs" in the organizational hierarchy. In more concrete terms, software's integration has affected the everyday worklife of programmers in different ways, according to their place in the organization. Regardless of where they

[2]Where one might have expected the most useful analyses of workplace organization—management literature—is precisely where the least material is found. Most is hortatory—not to say evangelical—rather than analytical or descriptive: managers should do such and such, try this or that technique, and so on. A good deal of it is simple huckstering. Occasionally, interesting things are found in the many publications of two very different management writers, Warren MacFarlen and Dick Brandon, both of whom have published extensively in various management and industry journals.

are, however, most software workers share a common workplace, even if they share it in different ways.[3] Perhaps the most striking aspect of the programmers' workplace is its physical separation from the computer. Programmers work in rooms or buildings—and sometimes even cities—where there is no hardware except for remote terminals. Even if they share the same room or building, the computer and the machine operators who run it are partitioned off and no one other than authorized machine-room personnel is allowed to enter the area.

It is hard to say with certainty why managers have done this. One reason, clearly, is security; it is a theme which appears regularly in management conventions and in industry and trade publications. Computers and their peripheral hardware are expensive. Accidental misuse or deliberate sabotage are too costly to risk uncontrolled, easy access to the machine room. Not only are the machines expensive, the products they make—the information they process—are usually vital to the smooth functioning of the organization. Interrupt the computer's work—or tamper with it—and the organization may be in great trouble.

But whatever the official reasons, separating the software worker from the machine, the machine room, and machine room employees constitutes the first and perhaps the most important of the head/hand separations he or she experiences in the data processing workplace (Greenbaum). The machine and its operation are, for the software employee, part of "production operations," and with these he or she usually has no direct involvement. Programmers may never set foot in the machine room or have casual contact with any of its employees. If they have any contact, it is almost always limited to appearing at a window—similar to a teller's cage—to give or get programs the machine will or has run. The contact is usually as swift and impersonal as a banking transaction, exchanging pieces of paper with a minimum of words. Sometimes there are complaints on one side about the slowness of service, sometimes

---

[3] What follows is an analysis of "the" software workplace. There is, obviously, no one such place. Both the nature of programming work and the form of the social relations among software workers will vary according to the kind of programming being done, the "product" being made, the use to which the product will be put, the hardware and software used, as well as the size, structure, and history of a specific organization.

But just as all bureaucracies share a number of characteristics no matter what their content or goal, programmers share to a remarkable degree common workplace experiences, relations to each other, and to nonsoftware workers. This is only appropriate in an occupation which has been the object of strenuous and occasionally frantic efforts to make it indistinguishable from other occupations and just as easily located in any bureaucratic organization.

from the other on the impatience or unreasonable demands on the part of the "customer."

If the partition between computer operators and programmers symbolizes the separation between hardware and software workers, the physical layout of the software workplace reflects the head and hand divisions among programmers themselves. At one point it was considered necessary to provide all software workers with private or semi-private offices, or failing that, with the omnipresent cubicles, partitioned spaces which afforded some privacy. This was the time, now gone, when even the lowliest software worker was considered, if perhaps a misanthrope, also a creative artist who needed quiet times and peaceful spaces to think and do his or her creative work. The effort to transform virtually all of the coding workforce and most applications programmers into clericals has been accompanied by a rearrangement of their "shop floor." In larger shops they are now placed in rows of desks, much like draftsmen or secretaries in a typing pool. In smaller shops, coders may share workplaces with other employees. These may be large and filled with many employees, including non-edp employees, or small rooms shared by just a few people.

The details of the spatial arrangement of software workers are the product of many factors, including matters of chance. An organization may intend to assign all software employees, including coders, semi-private offices or cubicles, but may be cramped for space and unable to do so. On the other hand, it may claim good intentions, but never for some reason get around to living up to them. In one workplace, for example, the official company policy was a department joke. All programmers were entitled to semi-private offices, but there was a perpetual "space shortage." The only people who actually got offices were "senior" programmers—all the senior programmers were somehow found office space in spite of the shortage, but no offices could ever be found for any of the junior software staff. Although the latter were in a room large enough to have their individual workspaces partitioned off, even that never happened. The result was a large room, filled with desks occupied by coders and junior-rank programmers, surrounded on all sides by glass-walled offices, each occupied by one or two managers, analysts, or senior programmers. The hardware was out of sight in a different building. Desks were clean except for loose-leaf binders and coding manuals, an occasional portable typewriter or hand calculator, and assorted personal oddments. Phones, remote terminals, and collections of software-related publications were kept in the managers' or analysts' offices. In most essentials, it was indistinguishable from an office of clericals in a large insurance company—except that clericals in those organizations are often given their own terminals.

If all software workers work in settings virtually identical to most other bureaucratic office places, like office workers, not all of them do the same things or experience the same relations with the same people. Each of programming's suboccupations has a unique set of social relations which must be examined separately. Let's start with the bottom of the programming ladder.

The programmer's day. If his or her physical surroundings are not significantly different from those of clerical workers in large organizations, the coder's work day (and that of the low-level programmer) is nearly as routine and unvarying. Unlike anarchic, unreconstructed individualists, coders and programmers—for that matter, almost all software workers—show up for work at about the same time of day and stay for about the same number of hours as clericals. Some may even punch a clock.

The first act each performs, after going to his or her desk (or punching in), is to have a cup of coffee. The act in itself is trivial but it also suggests something basic about the organization of the programmer's work and the nature of workplace relations. It indicates that in spite of routinization, programming, even coding, has not yet been completely remade to look like assemblyline work. Unlike line workers, programmers are not forced to adapt their physical motions to the rhythm and speed of a machine controlled by managers. Assembly line workers, once they punch in and take their place on the line, usually cannot deviate from a series of carefully structured motions. It is not just that they will be reprimanded by managers. If they omit an operation or take too long to perform it, the consequences are felt down the line by other workers: their behavior affects not only the product (and therefore the management), but their fellow workers. If employees are also on piece-work, their behavior on the line influences the ability of others to perform their assigned tasks, and thus incomes are directly affected. In clerical operations organized along the same principles of industrial mass-production workplaces, secretaries and typists are literally hooked into "word processing" equipment which not only provides them with work to be done, but automatically monitors and records their output to be used in evaluations by supervisors.

Coders and programmers—and software workers generally—are spared this sort of involuntary servitude to the machine, and, whether they think of it in such terms or not, the first cup of coffee in the morning is very much a symbolic statement of this independence. When they do begin their daily work routine, programmers usually do one of two things. They may look at the results of the latest computer run of their work, and evaluate its performance against the standards established for it. ''Evaluate'' is perhaps too strong a term. At this level of software work, tasks have been so routinized that the machine itself can be programmed to evaluate a given software fragment and generate ''error messages.'' It does much of the analytical work itself, in other words, leaving detailed correction to the coder.

That done, the coder or programmer may then look at the next task, given by a project leader or group manager. If the task is new or especially complex, the coder may discuss it with his project leader or an analyst or another coder. If there is little ambiguity about the assignment—if it is similar to coding jobs done many times before—the coder can sit down and begin writing code. Theoretically, this is what the programmer does all day, except for breaks and meals. Indeed, this is what managers like to see programmers do. Managers, according to one well-placed observer, assume that if pencil is not meeting paper, the programmer is slacking off (Weinberg). Staring at the wall can only be daydreaming, not constructive thought, since thinking is not a major component of low-level programming. Reading on the job is similarly not supposed to be part of the low-level programmer routine. Once trained, he or she is assumed to be more or less fully capable of performing the assigned tasks and therefore it should not be necessary to read anything, except perhaps coding manuals or reference volumes. Other reading, even if relevant to the programmer's job, is supposed to be done on the employee's own time. Programmers as clerks, in other words, are not expected to read—or to think—any more than the immediate job requires.

The routine of constant clerical labor does vary, however, and in practice few if any programmers or even coders spend entire days assembling program fragments the way autoworkers attach nuts to bolts. On the other hand, when the coding routine is broken, the interruptions are usually for one of a few predictable reasons. Because they are predictable, they also become routine and thus often formal parts of the programmer's or coder's schedule. There are conferences with project leaders, managers, and perhaps clients, usually people inside the organization. (Low-level programmers rarely talk directly with outside clients, except when in the company of the systems analyst or similar person who is defined as the "customer's man.") There may also be in-house training courses to attend, especially if new techniques are being introduced (see Chapter 3 on structured programming). There are, finally, the inevitable pep talks from managers at various levels. Other than that, the programmer works in a routine with surprisingly little daily variation.

In the course of doing their work, programmers may themselves occasionally be the cause of variations. Like the first cup of coffee in the morning, these variations are almost trivial but indicate the programmer's control over at least his or her physical motions. For example, in any group of programmers some will be more experienced or more skilled or more adept at a particular task. Or someone will have run into a particular coding problem that others have not yet encountered. Programmers as a matter of course act cooperatively. That is, when one confronts a problem or a difficult task, he or she will walk over to another programmer for help. The help, in turn, is routinely given. Thus a sort of master/apprentice heritage of the programmer as artisan persists even among the least skilled of the occupation. It also extends the possibilities of workplace control. For example, if a programmer works in a very large shop employing dozens or hundreds of software workers spread over several floors or even buildings, seeking advice and consultation from a more experienced programmer who works somewhere else holds all sorts of possibilities for re-arranging one's work schedule. Programmers who physically wander too often and too far, however, are soon suspected of wandering in other ways, notably devotion to work and job.

The analyst's day.   There is considerably more variation in the daily routine of the analyst because of the nature of his work and his varied social role. It might be more accurate to say, in fact, that there are two different kinds of software workers who are called analysts, each with somewhat different tasks, responsibilities, and patterns of workplace relations. The analyst's role as "conceptual architect" contains elements of both the technical specialist—the "super programmer"— and the managerial "generalist," the intermediary who works out the specifications set by the customer and which are to be met by the programmers who do the work. He can be, in other words, either a high-level technical expert or a go-between, depending on the workplace. Each kind of analyst leads a slightly different life (and, as we shall see in the next chapter, is likely to anticipate a very different career).

For the *analyst as expert,* the day begins, like the coder, with a cup of coffee. Unlike the coder, he is accorded the privacy of an office because his work is thought to be especially demanding. He consults colleagues frequently on technical matters (and is often consulted by less-skilled programmers and coders in turn). He often sits down in his office or in a library to read technical journals and reports. He makes more frequent use than coders of remote terminals and sometimes has access (if only informally) to the machine room and machine room personnel. He also gets company time off to attend industry or scientific conferences, and sometimes his work involves reporting on these trips to other software employees.

The *analyst as manager* leads a considerably more varied work life than either the coder or technical specialist. He, too, has his morning coffee, but rather than sitting in his desk or terminal or library chair to deal with problems of coding or design, he is likely to be off to the first of a long series of meetings with an assortment of people. These may include clients, managers, outside salesmen, and personnel department people, as well as the programmers who will produce the code. A great deal of time is spent talking with people: selling, cajoling, consulting on program design and specification, and so on, and much less on the nitty-gritty of writing code. Presumedly because he does so much officially sanctioned talking (as opposed to the merely tolerated, informal kind done by coders and programmers), the analyst/manager almost always has a private or semi-private office.

The analyst's office serves another function. Reference manuals, technical volumes, and remote computer terminals used by programmers are often in his office. Programmers thus show their symbolic as well as hierarchical subordination to him by coming in to use them. The visits I observed were almost always casual and informal: no discreet throat-clearing was ever necessary until permission to enter was granted. The standard exchange was a quick ''hi'' and ''see you later'' after the volume was retrieved or the terminal used. But however simple the ceremony, the relationship is unmistakable.

Actually, there may be no one in the analyst's office to even grant permission to enter. The analyst's day may involve (after the first cup of coffee, of course) early morning meetings or out of town trips to management and industry conferences and conventions. He may be asked to interview potential employees or employees bidding on openings in his department. All of these activities, of course, are considered part of the analyst's job responsibilities, and few questions are raised about the frequent and regular absences from his nominal workplace, his frequent physical movement, or other forms of ''socializing.''

Software's marginal man: The programmer manager. Except in the smallest "shops," programmers are usually divided into groups defined by job task or bureaucratic-organizational function. Whether "line" or "staff," the groups are further subdivided into "project" groups. The extent of the subdivision varies with such things as complexity of the task, skill of the software workers in the group, and the bureaucratic traditions of the department or even the parent organization itself.

Like other mind-work forced to adapt and subdivide itself in response to bureaucratic workplaces, programming has presented managers and administrators with major problems with respect to establishing "lines of authority." The problem, common enough in engineering and scientific bureaucracies, is compounded because programming is still very much in a state of flux, still being "shaken down" in order to establish clear-cut divisions of labor and job descriptions, both of which are necessary pre-conditions for establishing who is in charge of what and whom.

In an occupation so amorphous, whose suboccupations are so vaguely defined and which inevitably overlap, each workplace will define its workers' tasks somewhat differently. It will also arrange them differently. In concrete terms, it means different supervisory arrangements will be tried in different workplaces, and even in the same workplaces, simultaneously or sequentially, until an arrangement satisfactory to managers has been found. Until—and if—software work is made to be like other mass-production industrial labor, we can anticipate regular experimentation by managers trying to adjust their workplaces in such a manner that will afford them the desired combination of production and control.

But programming has already been subjected to a degree of fragmentation and de-skilling and it has been inserted, more or less comfortably, into the most bureaucratized of workplaces. Thus, while there is still considerable variety and continued experimentation with workplace organization, a general pattern has emerged, based on long-tried arrangements in the older engineering industries. Here, of course, programming's electrical engineering heritage has been crucial in showing managers the way. Software managers have borrowed from engineering workplaces two somewhat different, if related, supervisory modes. One utilizes people highly skilled in the work tasks being performed. Senior specialists provide experienced help and guidance to less experienced workers. Essentially an updated form of the master/apprentice model, it should be considered "technical supervision" rather than "management" in its common sense. The people who perform these technical supervisory tasks may be called by a variety of titles, according to their particular workplaces: "lead programmer" or "senior programmer" or even "chief programmer." Occasionally they may also have the title of systems analyst, but this seems rare and becoming more so.

The other form of supervision—workplace administration—is an explicitly social, i.e., control, function rather than a matter of technical guidance of the production process. These supervisory workers—now officially called managers—typically are responsible for assigning subtasks to group members and making sure the individual members and the group as a whole meet assigned deadlines and standards established by higher-level managers. They also keep tabs on group members: evaluating performance and attitudes, recommending pay increases, promotions, and so on. They often have final authority over who will be hired or transfered in or out of their groups.

Project managers, in turn, report to managers of their own. Where and who these higher-level managers are depend, of course, on the size of the organization, the size of the software workplace, the nature of the software being produced, and a large number of other variables. In theory, the levels may be endless, but generally, intermediary levels of software management integrate the products of the project groups below them, e.g., "assembling the modules."

At some point, the highest-level managers can be considered to be performing executive rather than supervisory functions. In other words, they make policy, not management (production) decisions: they, not the managers, make use of the software produced by programmers, either for internal use by the organization or to sell to a customer. Their titles reflect the difference. They can be "Head, Management Information Systems" or "Vice-President, Information and Administration" or in some situations simply "Manager, Data Processing."

In few workplaces known to me are the divisions between technical and administrative supervision so neatly drawn as they are described here, especially at the level where the code is actually written or where program designs are constructed. In fact, technical, analytical, and worker control tasks tend to be assigned to the same person. The chief programmer concept—which is essentially a combination of the lead (or senior) programmer and manager—represents an attempt to formalize precisely this sort of arrangement. In practice, supervisors are either primarily technical specialists or primarily conventional management "generalists" according to the peculiar circumstances of their workplaces.

The ambiguity of their positions has made software supervisory employees marginal people in several respects. If technical overseers, their role makes them foremen—neither employees nor managers. They are subject to conflicting pressures from their colleagues on the one side and from conventional managers on the other. If they are primarily managers rather than technical specialists, their personal dilemma can be even more acute. They are put in software workplaces to play not simply a technical role, but a socially superior one. Yet, they come to their positions in a questionable way. Seldom are they technically more skilled than the people they supervise. Indeed, one of the frequent complaints voiced by programmers about their project or group managers is that they are technically illiterate. The charge cannot be taken literally, but it does indicate a lack of respect for the technical competence of the people who pass judgment on their performance, who oversee the work process, and who represent the group and its members to the outside world.

The programmer manager's dilemma is especially obvious at low bureaucratic levels, e.g., coding and applications programming. Here there is little real managing for the manager to do, in part because the work is so structured it forces programmers to work in a certain way or because it allows the machine to monitor a programmer's performance. Even in matters of pay and promotion, the manager's authority is severely limited (see Chapter 5). In these workplaces he becomes little more than a strawboss, one who may see his position eliminated even before coders and applications programmers by new social or technological innovations.

After hours

It seems appropriate to conclude this discussion of workplace relations by describing what software workers do after quitting time, that is, to what extent the workplace follows the software worker home. As might be expected, different kinds of software workers are affected in different ways. Systems analysts, whether "super programmers" or conventional managers, very often do come in earlier and stay longer than the people they manage. They also come in on their days off, especially if there is a deadline to meet. Managers frequently take work home to complete: there are reports to read or write, technical articles to go over, correspondence, or anything else not attended to during the day.

Some extra-hours work may be anticipated and compensated. For example, if deadlines are close, managers may be required to spend 12 or 14 hour days or longer to get the work done. Because they are salaried, compensation seldom takes the form of extra salary payments, although bonuses are a common practice in some private industries. More typical is an unofficial day off during a slack period. Some companies present managers with small gifts—a complimentary dinner at a local restaurant, a month's membership at a local athletic club, and so on.

Sometimes the work is unexpected and uncompensated. In an interview, one project manager told me of an episode which took place shortly after he had been promoted to his present post:

When I first became a manager, one of the other [managers] gave me all sorts of advice. One of the things he said was never stay around town during my vacation and let everybody know long before I left that I was making big plans. Well, I didn't think anything about that and when vacation time came around I had forgotten he ever said anything. That year I just decided to stay home and add a room to the house and fix my boat. Well, sure enough, my manager calls not two days after and tells me they're way behind and they need me and I'd better help out.
. . . . Ever since then, I've made sure we have been somewhere else.

On the other hand, some extra-curricula assignments can be pleasant for managers. They can expect that part of their routine will include management conferences, industry conventions (like those sponsored by the National Computer Conference or the Association for Computing Machinery), as well as smaller commercial seminars offered by professional consultants. Employers have decided that such meetings are useful and managers are regularly sent to them and have their expenses—registration fees, hotel, and other expenses—paid for by the employer. In my experience, some of these conferences have been serious occasions attended by earnest, attentive people. Others were commercial road-shows of traveling "experts" selling an act, a common phenomenon in management and industry circles. Whatever their nature, they offer some managers a company-paid trip away from their workplaces and an opportunity to meet other people in the same field.

Analysts, managers, and high-level specialists put in longer work days, take their work home with them, and go off to work-related meetings. The demands and (in the case of conventions and out of town meetings) the rewards of their jobs reflect the supervisory nature of their work and the socially dominant position of their role. The after-hours relationship of coders (and low-level programmers) to their workplaces also reflects the social place of their work and their on the job social relations with other software workers. Few coders or low-level programmers take work home with them, unless enrolled in a training program. Except for maintenance programmers (who act as fix-it men for programs and who are told that dead of night calls are a mandatory part of their jobs), few put in extra hours unless compelled to do so. As their work has been made to look like conventional industrial work and their workplaces arranged accordingly, low-level software employees have responded by thinking and acting like production-line workers. The response can be surprisingly self-conscious and deliberate, as reflected in the following exchange in an interview with an applications programmer:

Q. Do you ever think about your work when you go home?
A. No, not really. I used to, when I started working, but not now.
Q. Why?
A. Well, it's a sort of personal thing, with respect to my manager. . . . See, we're supposed to be in by 8:12 and I'm not a morning person so it's hard. Anyway, my manager mentioned this, really casual at first, no big deal. But after a couple of times more, he got very short, you know. Well, after he started making nasty noises, I showed up at 8:12, right on the button instead of 8:20 or 8:30 or whatever it was. But now I leave at 5:06 on the button, instead of staying later. . . .
Q. You mean you used to stay after quitting time?
A. Oh, sure. I mean, if I'm working on something and I'm in the middle, I don't like to stop what I'm doing just because of what the clock says. Now I do. . . .

To summarize, the social organization of the software workplace is distinguished by its similarity to not its differences from other white-collar occupations in mass-production industrial organizations. Technical specialists are assigned the responsibilities of "mind-work," while most others are employed to take care of the mass of detail labor. Relations between mind-worker and detail worker are not as rigid as in other occupations, however, because the work itself has not been easy to fragment and because in some workplaces, especially small ones, there are no pressing reasons to create artificial divisions.

There is, nonetheless, a hierarchy. It is confused, it overlaps, and it will undoubtedly change several times as managers try to make the software workplace look even more like, say, a "word processing" typing pool, populated by clericals and their managers. Coders will experience even more efforts to organize them like clerks, analysts will find themselves acting more and more the role of salesman as well as technical specialist, while low-level managers will experience great pressures to eliminate their jobs altogether.

The efforts of higher-level managers to move software workers in this direction are graphically expressed in the way software career paths have been structured, salaries determined, and even how programmer attitudes have been shaped and given direction by managers. All of these are examined in the next chapter.

References   Greenbaum, Joan (1976). Division of labor in the computer field. *Monthly Rev.,* 28, 3: 40–55.

Hebden, J. E. (1974). Patterns of work identification. Salford, England: University of Salford (mimeo).

Pettigrew, Andrew M. (1973). Occupational specialization as an emergent process. *Soc. Rev.* 21, 2:233–278.

Weinberg, Gerald M. (1971). *The Psychology of Computer Programming.* New York: Van Nostrand Reinhold.

5 The programmer's workplace: Part II careers, pay, and professionalism

Introduction Programming, more than any other engineering occupation, has a reputation as an open field in which advancement, if not certain, is likely and the rewards substantial. Part of the reputation is based on fact. The men and women who created the computer and software industries have been part of one of the great occupational booms of the twentieth century. The pioneers of the 1940's and 1950's benefited from being first in a field which appeared to have no limits on its growth and therefore no limits on the opportunities for those with skill, talent, and ambition. Still prominent in a variety of occupations, their individual and collective careers have been held up as models for succeeding generations of software workers.

But the conditions which made rapid personal success possible no longer exist, at least not for most contemporary software workers. As a result of the sustained efforts of several generations of managers, career possibilities now clearly reflect programming's integration into conventional organizational structures. We have already seen the effects of this in the division of the work itself: "creative" work is separated from "clerical" work while the latter has been further subdivided into detail labor. Now that the work is thoroughly fragmented, the rewards and opportunities associated with the work have undergone a parallel fragmentation. The most obvious consequence has been the creation of at least three separate software careers—coding, programming, and systems analysis/management—where there had been one.[1] To the ex-

[1] A recent trend has been *to collapse* the distinction between people called programmers and people called systems analysts into a single category called "programmer/analyst." However, in workplaces where everyone is called "programmer/analyst," invariably grade qualifiers are found, e.g.,

tent formal training for each becomes more standardized and the recruitment into each becomes more dependent on formal credentials, it is less and less likely that software careers will begin with coding, progress to "programming," and from there continue to analysis. Instead, "career paths" are likely to proceed more or less exclusively *within* the major suboccupations.

Already there are some indications of this. Each of the major suboccupations has come to be characterized by a multitude of slightly different job descriptions, each with a slightly different pay range and set of working conditions. Work fragments differ according to detail, not task content or even skill. Furthermore, differences in job descriptions—and the pay usually associated with them—are based on formal criteria such as education credentials and seniority rather than on the nature of the work or the competence of the worker. Ironically, the proliferation of slightly different job titles and descriptions has come about when there are fewer rather than more real opportunities for career advancement. These, furthermore, are increasingly concentrated in the suboccupations with the fewest workers, that is, among analysts and other supervisory workers. Indeed, it seems likely that arbitrary and artificial divisions have been manufactured by managers to provide the appearance of career opportunities just as real opportunities shrink, particularly for new entrants at the lowest skill levels.

Like the fragmentation of the work itself, the fragmentation of careers has been used by managers to fill jobs with people acceptable to them and to make managing them easier. Pay and promotions, after all, are more than just rewards for work well done. They are devices of control. They structure recruitment, shape employee aspirations, and manipulate workplace behavior. The suboccupations, in other words, have been subjected to a process of *social* subdivision: more or less the same kind of work has been given a variety of job titles in order to reward different kinds of people in different ways.

Software managers have—once again—simply appropriated a morale-boosting technique developed and refined by the traditional engineering industries. It is by now an old, well-established management device. Technical employees are placed in job categories which are associated with specific pay ranges, privileges, and even symbols of "rank" such as telephones, private offices, rugs of various shades, etc. Such rewards, of course, can be labeled "promotions" when accom-

---

"programmer/analyst, level 3." In addition, there is usually a *de facto* functional division. Someone emerges as the main debugger, another the main documentation specialist, and some are burdened with most of the maintenance, etc. See Conger.

panied by a shift in work task or change in workplace. Many such "promotions" can then be put together to form a "career."

The technique, in short, is designed to allow managers to channel "acceptable" people into "appropriate" jobs. Those considered good workers can be rewarded with "advancement" from one fragment to another essentially identical to it but with a higher rank and perhaps a carefully regulated salary increment. Those exhibiting fewer management-approved virtues can be warned to improve their attitudes and performance by holding back career and income.

Careers for coders and low-level programmers

Artificial promotions are used in different ways in the different software suboccupations. More concretely, the head/hand separation has put different limits on the ranks managers can convincingly construct for coding, programming, analysis, and even management occupations. Coders and low-level applications programmers predictably confront the most restricted set of career opportunities. The training of low-level software workers is narrowly vocational and heavily ideological, that is, coders learn not only what they are expected to do for their entire working career and to accept without question the reason for doing it, but the right of superiors to tell them what to do. They are explicitly discouraged from exploring questions or issues beyond their assigned tasks. Programmers are praised when they stick to their assigned, narrow roles. Virtue is turned into vice, however, if programmers ever question the wisdom (or competence) of their managers. Their training provides them with only a limited view of the "Big Picture," and therefore managers can claim programmers are neither capable nor entitled to make decisions beyond those specifically assigned to them.

If the training of programmers deprives them of the opportunity to confront larger tasks, the structure of most organizations puts additional limits on their ability to find more interesting or more responsible or simply different kinds of work. Unless coders are able to switch occupations, that is, unless they consciously attempt to abandon coding and enter technical programming, sales, or management occupations, their career possibilities are as limited as other production or clerical workers. The most they can reasonably anticipate is movement from one work detail to another, a process which Fischer and Lesser call "serial fragmentation" when it occurs among traditional engineering workers. Such career advancement—hardly more than a formalization of periodic pay increments—is for managers primarily a bookkeeping device to account for differential pay based on seniority or formal credentials.

Coders and applications programmers will occasionally experience a real, rather than apparent, enlargement of both work tasks and career opportunities. Some movement always takes place and it is a rare organization which does not encourage a degree of in-house recruitment and promotion "through the ranks." But it is unlikely for present-day coders to be recruited through the ranks to more than straw-boss status (however formally designated). Promotion to higher positions in (technical) programming or in analysis and management usually requires more training, more credentials, or both. Sometimes in-house training or company-subsidized educational opportunities are available to coders and applications programmers to "upgrade" their skills. Here real chances for significant, rather than superficial, job changes are possible for some individual software workers. (But see Chapter 6, pp. 104–106.)

For the most part, however, coders confront horizontal rather than vertical movement. Deprived of all but the most narrow skills and of an understanding of how their work fits into the work process as a whole, low-level software employees can anticipate periodic shifts from one fragment to another until they are replaced by younger people who will do the same work for less money—or until the software and hardware industries succeed in their quest to eliminate coders completely.

Careers for managers   We have already discussed the two supervisory modes which have developed in the programming workplace: one based on technical expertise and assigned to technically sophisticated analysts or other expert employees such as "software scientists," the other more explictly social in nature and assigned to people with training or skills in people manipulation. In practice, both formal training and workplace responsibilities overlap. Specialists perform managerial/control roles while managers must possess a degree of technical expertise in order to perform their duties. The dual nature of supervisory work contributes to a lengthening of the career possibilities available to both kinds of supervisory workers. The career opportunities are somewhat different for each, however, and just as it was useful to divide the analysis of the work day into several parts, so is it useful to look at supervisor careers separately, Here we look at the career paths available to supervisory workers whose jobs are primarily social rather than technical, that is, "managers."

There may have been a time when programmer managers were simply skilled programmers who were also skilled in helping fellow programmers overcome technical problems. Not for a long time, however, has the management of programmers been left to such happy accidents of individual personality. Software management has received intense, systematic study by the industry; it is necessary only to recall the SAGE project to underscore the long-standing concern with formal management techniques. Since then, edp and software management has been constituted a distinct suboccupation in programming, even if its boundaries and specific duties are as vague as the other software occupations.

Managers come to their jobs with different kinds of preparation. Some may have been trained initially as technical experts—programmers, electrical engineers, even systems specialists—and then made the transition to management via promotion to low-level supervisory jobs, for example, as a project leader or as "chief programmer." Prior to or shortly after this initial step, they often take in-house management training courses or similar courses offered by local educational institutions in order to improve their abilities to "motivate employees."

Others are trained as managerial "generalists" and have acquired experience or formal training in software or electronic data processing. In this case, the chief purpose of their technical expertise is to provide managers with sufficient background to formulate production or policy questions or to make management (or "executive") decisions which involve the use of computers. Their training is largely a stepping-stone to a nontechnical career path. "Generalists" are trained for and are expected to see themselves aiming towards careers manipulating people, ideas, and situations, not technical information. Managers with technical training—as opposed to the technical specialist with some management training—are poised to leave behind the technical aspects of "software production" and to move to positions of broader decision-making responsibilities. They are trained, in other words, so they can move from the management of a small group of programmers to the management of an entire "shop" to a whole organization which includes non-data-processing divisions.

Of the two, the advantages clearly lie with the technically knowledgeable manager rather than the technical specialist who manages other specialists. Project managers, while clearly in a better position than coders, share one aspect of their career possibilities. They confront their own version of "serial advancement," promotions from one project to another, while higher management and executive positions are limited to "generalists" with the "appropriate" training.

Additionally, only generalists can make use of career possibilities outside conventional organizations. Opportunities have been extended by the emergence of related occupations which have sprung up to service the software, edp, and computing industries. The extensive overlap between training institutions and industry, for example, has provided "generalist" managers with opportunities to become academics in schools of management and engineering institutions. Similarly, managers with wide contacts in their industries are sometimes in a position to go into business themselves as consultants or software entrepreneurs, selling packaged software or personnel evaluation techniques or any of a wide range of other services. Some large companies will occasionally subsidize their managers or executives in these undertakings, either as bookkeeping devices (for example, to reduce taxes or simplify accounting procedures) or as experiments to test new products or services without directly involving the parent company.

Still other sources of career opportunities available primarily to "generalists" are the trade and industry journals and newsletters, as well as occupational and industry organizations which require people with both managerial experience and extensive social contacts in the industry. They become salespeople, lobbyists, business managers, and occasionally writers and editors.

A minor but intriguing career opportunity available to some enterprising software specialists is the traveling road show. These are commercial seminars or lectures sponsored by companies, trade groups, management associations, or even by the traveling entrepreneurs themselves. They consist of lectures or discussions led by "experts" in various aspects of programmer management. The lecture/discussions may be semi-technical in nature (a popular recent topic was structured programming and how to overcome resistance to it from the software staff) or concerned with more conventional management issues such as software security or evaluating programmer "productivity" or establishing "standards." Sometimes they are hardly more than the traditional exercises in moral uplift that management gatherings are so fond of. [At one conference, sponsored by an association which considers itself a serious group doing non-frivolous things, the speaker, complete with overhead projector, transparencies, blackboard, etc. began the lecture with: "The major function of managers is to manage." A slide was produced which read, "The major function of managers is to manage." Everyone in the audience—made up of managers—carefully copied down this injunction. After a suitable period to allow the slower scribes to complete their task, another, equally direct, injunction was pronounced accompanied by its own slide. This, too, was dutifully transcribed by everyone present. The lecture went on in this manner and at this pace for fifteen minutes, followed by one almost identical to it. I have attended other inspirational meetings for managers which were somewhat more original and lively, but not much.]

Careers for technical specialists

''Super programmers'' are software's equivalent of traditional engineers; they do neither the routine work of the technician nor the direct supervisory work of conventional managers. They also occupy a middle position with respect to career opportunities. More skilled than managers or coders in software design and writing, they confront some of the possibilities and limitations of each. If supervisors and low-level programmers hardly ever cross career paths, for technical specialists who constitute the core of most ''shops,'' the situation is much more fluid.

In part, the nature and extent of career opportunities will reflect the emphasis of the specialist's work. For some systems analysts, whose job tasks make them go-betweens for client and producer, the transition to full-fledged supervisory or ''executive'' work can be relatively straightforward. On the other hand, analysts who are primarily technical experts confront a classic dilemma. The organizations which employ them are organized as hierarchies. Each hierarchical position represents both a different level of responsibility and a distinct career step. This sort of institutional arrangement makes sense only when advancement is defined as moving from a position of less authority and control to another with more, that is, it makes sense for management occupations and for armies. Technical and scientific occupations, on the other hand, are not inherently amenable to military-like separation of substantive job tasks or to authority distinctions based on them. An engineer may be more or less experienced, more or less senior, or even more or less competent, but he or she is either an engineer or something else which is not an engineer.

Technical specialists have as a consequence presented managers with the problem of inserting unconventional employees into conventional bureaucratic structures which were designed for detail workers and the managers of detail workers, but not for people who are neither.

One solution is simply to attach different titles to the same work and associate each title with slightly different pay. Specialists can find themselves called ''senior'' programmers or ''staff'' programmers or some variation of these, e.g., ''junior staff programmer,'' which in turn can be stretched, when necessary, with qualifiers, e.g., "associate senior programmer." The titles do not represent changes in the actual production, workplace, or social role of the programmer. They indicate only management efforts to provide the appearance of a technical career path which resembles the well-established—and real—career paths of managerial and sales employees. The construction of a technical career "ladder," in other words, is a variation of a long-standing management device known as the "dual ladder," yet another borrowing from the management repertory of morale-boosting techniques. In practice, the technical "ladder" is considerably shorter than the "parallel" ladder for managers. Promotions can have little to do with changes in work performed; they must instead be based on increasingly fine distinctions of social attributes, like formal credentials. But differences in job title and rank based on length of service or school degrees, however finely subdivided, eventually run out. At this point the technical specialist has reached the end of his or her "career ladder" and must deal with the possibilities of changing occupations or coming to a dead-end and probable "obsolescence."[2]

Unlike coders, technical specialists are in a good position to make career changes, but only if they are willing to abandon the technical aspects of software or use their technical knowledge and experience in explicitly management applications. If the specialists are systems analysts, they can readily emphasize the managerial component already present in their work. For them, the transition can be made with relative ease. If technically oriented, the transition may be harder, but technical specialists possess the formal credentials and experience sufficient social interaction with management to smooth the transition if they wish to do so. Their opportunities are enhanced by the steady demand for technically knowledgeable sales and management employees.

Pay   Perhaps the most significant feature of programmer salaries is their great range. By now this should not come as any great surprise. The work has been bureaucratically defined to include low-level clerical workers and high-level executives as well as technical specialists and middle-managers of all ranks. It is to be expected, therefore, that the extremes in wages would reflect such a division.

The 1975 *Datamation* survey provides one indication of how great the variation is—and how closely it parallels pro-

---

[2] For a discussion of management use of "dual ladders," see Goldner and Ritti.

gramming's fragmentation (Schlosky). The software respondants in this national survey were divided into two major categories: employees in self-contained data processing workplaces and employees in non-data-processing settings. Self-contained settings, that is, those workplaces which have been referred to here as "software shops," accounted for over 80 percent of the total. These in turn were divided into four software job "families" plus two "families" of management occupations. The six "families" in their turn were sub-divided into six rank-ordered levels: manager, lead, senior, Level A, Level B, and Level C, where Level C represented a new trainee. The survey also correlated each of the "families" with size of the workplace, defined by average monthly hardware rental.

(Software workers employed in nonsoftware workplaces were also divided into six categories, but they had to make do with only two "families": systems analysts and applications programmers.)

The 1975 salary range for conventionally organized software workers, that is, those who worked in "shops," was $129 to $505 per week among nonmanagerial employees and $177 to $764 per week for managers. There was considerable variation by size of installation as well as the expected variation according to the "rank" order of the job title. For example, in the lowest paid category—trainee systems programmers in the smallest shops—the range was $129 to $261, while for department managers in the largest organizations the range was $364 to $764.

The *Datamation* ranges were intended to provide managers and employees with a comparison of salaries based on installation size and type. Its use of five nonmanagement job levels was an effort to collapse the great variety of slightly different job descriptions found from workplace to workplace. The general descriptions, like the specific ones they are based on, are necessarily arbitrary and can provide little in the way of specific information. Even the ranges within each categorical level are ultimately of little help since the upper limits in most cases are almost twice as large as the lower, and there is considerable overlap between ranges. Moreover, in some software workplaces there are considerably more than the five job descriptions which comprise the *Datamation* job families. (In one shop I observed, for example, there were nine categories of programmer/analyst, and management was about to increase that to 16.) Obviously, there is a lot of room to maneuver, as well as to "advance."

More helpful than the job description salary ranges are the

survey's figures on salary increases/losses during the period 1970–1975. The results exactly parallel the social separation of software into managers, technical specialists, and clericals. During the period, applications programmers and programmer/analysts had the smallest percentage increase of software workers, while managers had the largest: about 33 percent compounded increase versus about 53 percent. Systems analysts were in the middle, with about 42 percent. These are unadjusted figures. Adjusting for inflation during the period, managers enjoyed a compounded gain of about 13 percent; analysts more or less kept even with a slight gain of about 2 percent; applications programmers and programmer/ analysts actually *lost* between 6 and 7 percent of their real incomes during the same period. (Systems programmers were not surveyed during the whole period and therefore no comparisons could be made.)

The *Datamation* survey indicates that nonmanagement programmers may earn low salaries for so glamourous an industry—as little as $7,000 per year—and the salary ranges vary considerably from one industry to another and from one organization to another. At the level of the individual organization, however, the variation is not as random as the national data make it appear. In shops maintained by all but the smallest organizations, a wage range is established for each job description. The range is structured to take into account such individual variations as length of employment, employee evaluations by supervisors, formal credentials, and so on. Often, special allowances are made for local conditions, e.g., a shortage or surplus of potential workers in a particular category which might force the organization to raise the ceiling limit or allow it to lower the floor.

The ability of managers to deviate from the approved range varies with the particular organization, job level, and job market. It is possible, however, to describe a general process commonly used for arriving at the salaries of coders and programmers. Managers are under great pressure to keep salaries as low as possible, for reasons which require no elaboration. On the other hand, there are counterpressures which may push salaries up. One such pressure is the steady demand for software workers, for the present still a seller's market. Another source of pressure comes from the shortage of people with high-level programming skills. Relatively few software workers, for example, design new operating systems or new languages, and as a result they command higher salaries than, say, applications programmers.

For the low-level applications programmer, the pressures

clearly favor managers, particularly as the work becomes progressively routinized and standardized. Salary increases are carefully plotted out ahead of time along well-defined intervals and within carefully specified ranges determined by the same personnel office which establishes the salary ranges for all other employees. By way of illustration, let us consider the "average" applications programmer hired after finishing a two-year electrical engineering program at a community college. The organization's job description may call for a salary range of, say, $9,100 to $10,400 for an inexperienced programmer, the variation due to such factors as formal training, local market conditions, how urgently the organization needs to fill the position, etc. The manager hiring the programmer may offer the prospective employee a salary close to the bottom of the range if he thinks he can get away with doing so, more if not. After eight or twelve months, the new employee is reviewed and his/her performance evaluated. A salary increment will then be calculated on the basis of the evaluation. For example, managers may be required to rank "acceptable" performance by quartiles or even deciles, with a dollar subrange specified for each; the final, actual increment is influenced by such other variables as formal credentials and length of employment or how long the employee has been in the same general job category.

By this time, of course, much of the "decision-making" function of the programmer's immediate manager has been taken over by the salary matrix chart supplied by the personnel office, leaving the manager with surprisingly little to say about the size of the programmer's raise.

(The same procedure is repeated at subsequent evaluation intervals and once again whenever someone moves into a new job category, e.g., from "programmer" to "programmer/analyst." The entire incremental evaluation process then starts again.)

It bears repeating that in all but very small organizations the process is very organized, very carefully calculated, and admits, in theory, of little variation. Even if a manager wants to reward an individual programmer, he is under pressure to keep wage costs as low as possible. For one thing, managers are sometimes given a total wage pool which they must divide among all their employees. Money to pay for an unusually large increment thus must come out of the total increment allowance—and therefore out of the increments of other programmers. If there is too great a discrepancy, the less favored programmers may rebel by demanding comparable raises—or by leaving. If managers want badly enough to do so, there are ways to get around the salary limits. One is simply to promote the programmer to a higher bureaucratic level. But managers have little incentive to do this. Personnel managers closely monitor promotions and step in when too many (and too many salary raises) are passed out. The programmer manager's own evaluation and increment depend on how well he meets his budget limits.

But what of the other side of the relationship? Are not managers under pressure from programmers to give out maximum raises? The answer, surprisingly, is no, or at least, not usually. The nature of the workplace organization makes it hard for programmers to understand how such fundamental matters as their incomes are determined. Programmers are treated by their employing organizations as employees of a particular category who are paid a given salary within a pre-determined range. From the perspective of employers, in other words, programmers are just employees. The programmer's immediate manager, as we have seen, often has relatively little discretion in exceeding organizationally set limits.

Programmers, particularly low-level programmers, are not in a position to understand how structured their employment is. In interviews, they typically report that their salaries are worked out personally in private negotiations with their mana-gers and as a result are reflections of their individual achieve-ments and their individual bargaining abilities. Managers make every effort to reenforce programmers' belief that salaries are largely individual affairs worked out between the programmer and his or her own manager. In the course of an interview with an applications programmer employed by a hardware manufac-turer, I asked about pay. Part of the exchange follows:

Q. Are you satisfied with your pay?
A. Well, you know, you never think you get enough, but I'm pretty happy with what I'm getting.
Q. Why? Do you think they're paying you what you're worth?
A. You never get paid what you're worth. (Laughs) But I'm pretty much satisfied.
Q. Why?
A. Well, I'm right in the middle of the salary range for my job description. As a matter of fact, I'm close to the top.
Q. What is the salary range?
A. What is the range? You know, I don't really know, exactly. I don't think I ever really thought about it.
Q. Then how do you know you're in the middle?
A. Well, I guess because after I got my last raise, my manager told me I was in the top half of the salary range.

Q. Have you asked other people in your job description what their salaries are in order to compare?

A. No, we're not supposed to. I mean, we're told not to because talking about such things is unprofessional for programmers. Of course, I did sort of ask around once when I started, informally I mean, people I knew. They were all getting more or less the same thing I was, so I assumed we were all pretty much in the same range.

Salary schedules are generally not made public below managerial levels. As we have seen, programming employees are discouraged from talking about pay at all—specifically from talking with co-workers about their salaries. It is inevitable, however, that at least some software employees will learn of its existence or simply suspect it from a comparison of their co-workers' salaries. If they discover that their salaries are significantly lower than what seems to be the norm, the salary schedule now serves another function: to cool out the disgruntled employee. A manager can, in cases of unusually low salaries, give the programmer a larger than usual dollar raise at the next increment. The raise may be considerable as a percentage of the programmer's base salary (programmers have told me of receiving 25 percent increments after complaining of low salaries), but because the base was low to begin with, such large raises hardly ever bring the programmer's salary past the upper limit for the job level. An important ritual accompanies such raises. Managers will claim that the salary disparity was an oversight or mistake and, with a plea for secrecy and appeals to confidentiality, the manager will show the programmer a salary chart, sometimes the real one, sometimes not. He will then "prove" to the unhappy employee that with the new raise the programmer's salary is now near the top of the range and represents the manager's very best efforts. Only the personnel office prevented an even higher increment. The programmer, glad to get the raise he or she feels is deserved, is also pleased by the confidence the manager has shown in him or her by revealing such sensitive information. For managers, such "confidences" are routinely placed with any employee deemed worthy of keeping who complains about being paid less.

A special sort of salary discrimination will conclude the discussion of pay. A common method of determining the exact increments is to add a specified percentage for formal credentials. In the same organizations, people doing the same work and whose attributes are otherwise the same will sometimes be paid very different salaries according to the type and number of post-high school degrees. The differential pay schedules are sometimes called "paying for potential" by management and reflect the expectation that technical employees with college degrees are more likely to advance than those without them. Specifically, it indicates the organization's anticipation that college-trained software workers are more likely to become managers or salespeople and are to be rewarded according to their (usually higher) salary schedules rather than that for technical personnel. Occasionally, the differential is discovered and produces resentment among software workers without college training. In response to a question about pay scales in her shop, a programmer complained about what she thought was favoritism towards college graduates:

A. . . . like just recently we had a lot of new people come in, maybe about ten, in our department. They're all four-year graduates and when they first came in they were all making more than me, which was a real bummer.

Q. Did you talk with anyone about that?

A. Yes. I went to my manager and asked him about it and he explained it to me that it only mattered when people got hired, that their pay, that it went by their education. And he said that it really didn't matter once you got in the door it went by your programming ability.

Q. Your manager said it only mattered initially, in terms of starting pay, but you were there over a year and a half [before the new people arrived] and they still made more than you?

A. Right, well, it was maybe two weeks after I went in to talk to him that I got a raise and my last raise before that came was a lot, according to how raises go.

Q. How do raises go?

A. Usually about ten percent, it seems like, from what I hear.

Q. That's annually.

A. Right. The first raise when I first got into programming was about 24 percent, which they told me was because I was making less being from manufacturing [i.e., production], they had to get me up to the level of programming. The raise he gave he said was the highest that he could, he couldn't go any higher, and I believe him. So, when I went in to ask him about it he asked me if I thought he could have given me more money and I said no and the next raise I got was the same amount and I believe it's the highest he could give me. It will take awhile, from what he tells me, to get me up. Now I make more than them. . . .

Q. Do you think you would have gotten that catch-up raise if you hadn't gone in to speak with him?

A. I really don't believe I would have, not that soon. . . .

Professionalism   We have not yet exhausted the arsenal of managerial techniques of control. Of these, perhaps the most intriguing is management's use of an ersatz professional ideology grafted onto a nonprofessional occupation in order to encourage its members to "act like professionals." We have seen what "acting like a professional" means when it comes to salary. How have managers been able to use professionalism as a device to control software workers? Part of the answer has to do with the historical origins of professionals and part has to do with the way managers have modified the original concept to suit their own ends.

The occupation most people have in mind when speaking of professionals is that of the physician. There is good reason for this. Physicians emerged as a distinct occupational group during the Middle Ages. In ways which are interesting but not important here, they gradually organized themselves into occupational organizations patterned after those of their fellow small tradesmen and artisans—the guild. All medieval guilds, whether of barbers, masons, weavers, or physicians, had a few basic functions:

(1) to restrict entry into the occupation
(2) to eliminate competitive practices among guild members
(3) to enforce monopoly control over the performance—and the rewards—of the services of guild members.

Medieval guilds were, in other words, made up of independent, self-employed entrepreneurs, *who defined not only the content of their work but the conditions under which it was performed.*

It is important to underline the implications of these historical roots of professionalism. They arose at least as much out of a desire to protect monopolistic privilege as a desire to extend useful knowledge and to protect it against charlatanism; they arose to protect the vested interests of what were essentially self-employed small businessmen, not highly skilled employees; and they ultimately helped reinforce great social divisions by providing vital services to those who could pay for them rather than those who simply needed them. By the nineteenth century, when the first body of scientifically based knowledge was only just starting to become part of the physicians' tools, the basis of their "professional" status already had been long established by virtue of their *political and economic,* not their occupational, skills. The physician's unique body of knowledge came last and least and was grafted onto an already existing guild. It was kept unique, furthermore, largely because physicians took great pains to ensure that it remained so.

The occupational organization of these small businessmen/physicians is largely irrelevant to programmers who are overwhelmingly employees. The image of the professional that edp managers have in mind is, not surprisingly, different in some significant ways from the historical reality. It should be clear why managers, even as they encourage "professionalism" for some software workers, can't really tolerate programmers who resemble the prototypical physicians. It would mean, in managerial terms, control over admission into the occupation through peer certification and licensing; it would mean, therefore, deliberately induced labor shortages, high wages, and, most importantly, surrender of workplace control to the "professionals" themselves.

Managers, logically enough, have therefore changed the definition of professional which, for them, has all the advantages of the old guild organization and none of its disadvantages. Professionalism for programmers as it has emerged in management literature means: the establishment of universal job descriptions and standards, formulated, of course, by managers; common training programs; and perhaps a common certification process similar to that found among traditional engineering employees. On the other hand, the managers' image of professionalism does *not* include certification by an authority controlled by the programmers' peers; it does not include, certainly, licensing, nor does it foresee under any circumstances making independent entrepreneurs out of software workers. Management's vision, in other words, is of a profession without professionals. Such a "profession" would allow managers to work both sides of the street. Job "performance standards" would be established—presumedly at high "professional" levels—but the standards would be set by managers. In short, the managers' notion of professional programmers is one which gives them and not the programmer the power to define what programming is.

In practice, management has found some creative ways of imposing its particular vision of professionalism on programmers. Chief among these is the fragmentation of programming tasks we have previously discussed: arranging the newly-created fragments into a hierarchy, and then holding up "advancement" from one fragment to another as the substance of a "professional career." Aside from whatever advantages it may or may not have for efficiency, increased productivity, and so on, the hierarchical division created in the software workplace supplies managers with a structure which looks like a logical career line for "professionalized" programmers. Managers can now have it both ways: the aspirations of programmers can be channeled along clear-cut—if arbitrary—career paths and managers have been given a device that enables them to make sure they will remain in charge of programming. Tasks have been broken down, while at the same time the hierarchical arrangement of the work fragments gives the manager his traditional carrot of controlling individual advancement in the organization.

In practical terms, managers have derived a major benefit from encouraging a sense of "professionalism" among their software employees. Unions have been kept out of virtually all programming workplaces, countering a widespread trend among other white collar occupations. In no small measure this has come about as a consequence of management's vocal insistence that "programmer professionalism" and unions do not mix. The result has been to impose on programmers all of the disadvantages of collective action by denying them the advantages of either unionization *or* genuine professional standing, and doing so in the name of individual advancement. It is an individualism of a peculiar sort, confined to programmers' self-images, while major decisions about the work they do, pay, and about their career prospects are settled for them in an impersonal way by thoroughly organized employers.

References   Conger, J. Daniel. Pitfalls and potentials for edp training. *Data Management* (November 1974), pp. 33 *ff*.

Goldner, Fred and R. Richard Ritti. Professionalization as career immobility, *Am. Soc. R.* 72, 4:489–502.

Schlosky, Daniel P. DP salary survey. *Datamation,* 22, 1: 73ff.

6 The routinization of computer programming

Introduction What is most remarkable about the work programmers do is how quickly it has been transformed. Barely a generation after its inception, programming is no longer the complex work of creative and perhaps even eccentric people. Instead, divided and routinized, it has become mass-production work parcelled out to interchangeable detail workers. Some software specialists still engage in intellectually demanding and rewarding work—people who are called by such names as systems engineers, analysts, or simply software scientists—but they make up a relatively small and diminishing proportion of the total programming workforce. The great and growing mass of people called programmers (as well as those who do software work but for a variety of reasons are called something else) do work which is less and less distinguishable from that of clerks or, for that matter, assembly line workers.

The transformation of programming is not the result of technological imperatives inherent in the logic of programming or computing. Programming has changed because managers, concerned about profits, have set about systematically and carefully to change it. It has happened before. Similar attempts to routinize work have been made by managers of the most diverse workplaces. The common denominator has been the desire to substitute less skilled and therefore less expensive workers for more skilled and more expensive workers. Harry Braverman, in his definitive study of the organization of the modern workplace, has cited one of the earliest and clearest management statements on the ",cheapening of labor," that of the English manufacturer and economics writer, Charles Babbage. In 1832, Babbage wrote:

... the master manufacturer, by dividing the work to be executed into different processes, each requiring different degrees of skill or of force, can purchase exactly that precise quantity of both which is necessary for each process; whereas, if the whole work were executed by one workman, that person must possess sufficient skill to perform the most difficult, and sufficient strength to execute the most laborious, of the operations into which the art is divided. (Quoted in Braverman, pp. 79–80.)

Braverman adds, "To put this all-important principle another way, in a society based upon the purchase and sale of labor power, dividing the craft cheapens its individual parts" (p. 80). (At least one and probably several reviewers will note the irony: this was the same Charles Babbage who, along with his friend, Lady Lovelace, designed a prototype of the modern computer. Good!)

Profits from the sale of a product are thus inseparable from the ability of the owner (or his hired manager) to *control* the manner in which a product is made. Fragmentation of work and de-skilling of workers facilitate both. Fragmentation allows managers to appropriate to themselves control over the actual production process. Control means work can be further broken up and redesigned to require workers with minimum skills, reducing labor costs and, in the neutral-sounding phrase of economics, "increase productivity." (Control of the workplace by redesigning the work helps increase profits in other ways. A standard production process ensures a standard result. It reduces the ability of the worker to vary the product, in other words, either through innovation or malice, i.e., "sabotage." It also reduces opportunities for theft, if only because few workers ever see a finished product to steal. And it provides work for managers and engineers who design routinized workplaces.)

Breaking up work into simple parts is most obviously done in "traditional" industrial workplaces. There is, however, no reason why the same principles cannot be applied to so-called intellectual work, although the particulars of the divisions will naturally differ. Schools, offices, banks, and engineering workplaces all have experienced analogous divisions which in turn have produced armies of faceless "white collar" workers possessing the most rudimentary of work skills. Even electrical engineering, the leading edge of much of the deskilling process, has been routinized in the same way. "Software production" is thus only the most recent but certainly not the most complex of the white collar occupations to be forced into conventional industrial moulds.

Management practice and the de-skilling of programmers

The specifics of de-skilling techniques can be grouped in two major categories, according to their emphasis:

(1) those efforts which are intended to change the actual work of programming in order to render it simpler and more routine and therefore allow the use of less skilled workers
(2) those efforts designed to legitimate such work changes in order to make them acceptable or palatable to software workers and to counter potential worker resistence.

Changes in work

The centerpiece of management efforts to de-skill programmers is structured programming. It is at the center of management efforts (along with hardware changes) not only because of what it does to the actual process of writing programs but because it symbolizes the seriousness of management efforts to standardize "software production." The principles of structured programming are straightforward. Structured programming methods impose restrictions on the number and type of logical procedures a programmer may use. The limitations on procedure are the intellectual equivalent of limiting the worker's choice of tools as well as the sequence of their use. There is a similar restriction, imposed by the "logic" of the structured programming technique being used, on the kind and quantity of information which may be called upon for calculation. This is similar to the restrictions placed on an industrial worker with respect to the choice of materials. For example, a worker assembling a television receiver is restricted to soldering a resistor on a chassis. The specific rating of the resistor as well as its location in the chassis is determined for the assembler by engineers. The assembler may not decide that the resistor should be of a higher or lower rating or that it should be soldered somewhere else.

Structured programming makes it possible to organize programming along the lines of industrial rather than craft production. In this case, what is standardized is not a material product like an automobile or a package of breakfast cereal or a bank statement. What is standardized is a mode of thought, a logic, a pattern of decision-making. Ultimately, however, the thought, logic, and decision must take palpable form. Usually, the form is a document, the result of the programmer's writing down the symbols which represent choices he or she has made about code, instructions, data, and so on. The final goal of all programming must be these concrete (or paper) products of the programmer's activity.

To aid in the production of a standardized product, structured programming as a way to structure work has been complemented by various social arrangements to structure the relationships between software workers. The most important of these, discussed in some detail in Chapter 3, are "modular programming" and "Chief Programmer Teams." Both are extensions of structured programming principles to the level of workplace organization. To put it differently, modular programming and Chief Programmer Teams are attempts to define where programming is done and by whom, while structured programming defines how it is done. The organizational principles are the same: larger tasks are divided up into components, which are then assigned to workers on the basis of skill, experience, position in the organizational hierarchy (status), or some combination of these. In the Chief Programmer Team, the major divisions are between the "conceptual architect" and his assistants and the people who actually write the code. The latter are the equivalent of detail workers in conventional industrial workplaces or the "technicians" in conventional engineering workplaces. The divisions, in other words, are those between "mind" workers and "hand" workers. Modularization carries the process a step further and establishes divisions between the "hand" workers themselves. The detail workers are assigned "modules" which from the viewpoint of production engineers are identical to subassemblies in manufacturing workplaces. The modules—designed by "high-level" specialists and constructed according to the guidelines of structured programming—can be assembled, tested, and repaired independently of each other. A whole "system" can be structured to operate at all times (although at reduced capacity) while individual modules are checked for errors or replaced by new modules designed to alter the performance of the larger system.

In terms of the social structure of the workplace, modular programming is simply a fancy term for parcelling out standardized and relatively simple fragments to different work groups. Chief Programmer Teams are ways of organizing the work groups internally and of arranging them in a (management) desired relationship to each other. They define relations of power and therefore provide the basis for establishing formal hierarchies of rank as well as of function.

Other developments have played their parts in the reorganization of programming work, notably the growing use of prepackaged (or "canned") software and the creation of "smart machines" made possible by engineering and language advances. These have, singly and in combination, allowed managers to replace skilled software specialists with less skilled "applications programmers" and even with machine operators who have little or no software training. Important as these developments are, their profitable use depends on the ability of managers to standardize the making of programs, not just their consumption.

Legitimation techniques and propaganda

No one likes to see his or her skills made "obsolete" or to have the opportunity to make decisions about his or her work taken away and given to someone else. People, in these circumstances, are apt to get unhappy and resentful. What is also true—and very important to managers—is that people may resist efforts to reduce them to extensions of machines someone else had designed. As a result, managers (including in this case, personnel managers, consultants, and assorted "human relations" experts, as well as programmer and edp managers) have had to devise ways to convince software workers that de-skilling techniques are reasonable in themselves or, failing that, are at any rate the prerogatives of employers.

In a sense, this is merely carrying out the most fundamental role of all management workers, in the software workplace or any other. Managers earn their keep by trying to extract what they can from workers through various forms of supervision *and* by constantly claiming the moral as well as legal right to do so. Because engineers are able to redesign work tasks so that more and more workers effectively supervise themselves as they do their jobs, the functions of supervisory workers have become more ideological than ever. They have increasingly tended to concentrate on techniques of legitimation, that is, on promoting through various forms of propaganda the "inherent" right of managers and owners to control not only what the workers make, but where, when, and now even how they make it.

The legitimation campaign begins early, even before the software worker becomes an employee—or, for that matter, before he or she becomes a software specialist. I have tried to show in Chapter 2 how the training of software workers at all levels is organized to impart considerably more than specific or general skills. It is also organized to encourage programmers to accept the segmented nature of their work and the hierarchical structure of the organizations which employ them. They are encouraged to identify corporate profitability with technical rationality, technical rationality with efficiency, and their own individual success and advancement with the success of their future employers. Since advancement in most workplaces means gaining approval of immediate supervisors, they learn that advancement hinges on not just doing what a supervisor orders, nor even on accepting without question the right of the supervisor to order it. They come to understand that advancement requires they identify with the goals and expectations of the organization, i.e., of the owners and managers. Paradoxically, they must identify their goals with those of the people whose own job it is to simplify the programmer's work so that he or she eventually can be replaced by less skilled and cheaper workers. The goals they must identify with—job simplification and deliberately induced "obsolescence"—are intended to allow managers to get rid of employees, not promote them.

The organization of the workplace confirms and reinforces the lessons learned in school. Of the many devices employers use to establish their "right" to define both the software product and the manner of its making, three deserve emphasis. They are direct company propaganda, a more vague but also more pervasive ideology of individualism, and the encouragement of a management-defined programmer "professionalism."

Company propaganda is the most obvious as well as the most direct means of encouraging programmers to accept the loss of skill and control. It can take many forms, although perhaps the most typical are sessions ironically called "skill upgrading" classes. Sometimes new skills which represent genuine enlargements over what was known before are learned. On the other hand, when structured programming or similar techniques are on the agenda, such skill "upgrading" courses are in fact skill degrading exercises designed to cool out workers who correctly sense that they are about to lose something they already have: the ability to decide within broad limits how they will go about designing programs and writing code. So extensive is this direct propaganda effort that consulting firms which do nothing but cool out suspicious software workers are in constant demand for their particular service. Some hardware makers, committed to structured programming and similar "modularized" approaches to the "man-machine interface," also loan instructors to hardware customers to perform essentially the same tasks.

More subtle because it relies on internal regulation is management's encouragement of "individualism." Normally, individualism would be expected to promote resistance to management's claim that it has the right to control work. But this is an individualism of a peculiar sort, one which encourages personal success in the most collectivized of settings. "Individualism" means doing what anyone in a higher position tells you to do simply because he is in a higher position and can influence your chances for advancement. It is not an individualism of striking out on one's own, but of taking one's place. Managers implicitly recognize the contradictory nature of their appeal to "individualism" by advising their employees to seek personal advancement by "getting on board" or becoming a "team player." In practical terms, the legitimacy managers claim for their control of how programming is done is based on a deal, the terms of which are partly stated and partly implied: accept our (management's) right to tell you how to do your job and we will help you prosper. What is left unsaid is that doing what you're told may eventually mean accepting a trivialization and perhaps even total elimination of the employee's work.

The most vivid form of this anonymous and compliant individualism is, of course, programmer "professionalism." There is little agreement, in these times of rapidly changing work and workplaces, what, exactly, professionalism is. There is no doubt, however, what programmer managers mean by professionalism. It is a code of behavior to be adhered to by programmers but drawn up by their employers. The traditional features of professional organization and ideology—peer control of admission, training, prices, and sphere of power—are omitted and replaced with an inventory of acceptable and unacceptable behavior. Properly internalized by employees, such a code relieves managers of the necessity to directly supervise minute by minute behavior of software workers. An internalized "professional" ideology, in other words, replaces the conveyor belt and the foreman.

Predictions and other essays in prophesying

What can be said about the future of programming and the organization of the programming workplace? Almost certainly the process of work fragmentation and programmer de-skilling will continue and intensify. Fragmentation and de-skilling, in turn, will mean further changes in what kinds of people do the various subtasks which together make up "software production."

With respect to the work itself, it seems safe to anticipate that the proportion of "clerical" tasks to complex work will increase. More time will be spent in routine coding as the head and hand separation between software design and software production is applied to even the most elaborate of software writing. Canned programs and improvements in hardware will also contribute to the "clericalization" of programming.

But programming will become progressively routinized only because some programming work will become increasingly complex and demand the most elaborate of skills. The design of operating systems, of high-level languages, of the logic wired into the machines, the breaking up of work into sub-tasks, and other work directed towards coordination and supervision of detail labor will remain critical parts of future data processing. The major exception among supervisory tasks will likely be low-level management which will be taken over by machines. The success of the fragmentation process leaves the software detail worker so little discretion in the writing of code or the design of a program that direct supervision by a manager is unnecessary.

Changes in programming work will bring changes in the structure of the software workforce. Almost certainly, as the amount of detail work increases, so, too, will the number of software detail workers. They will be hired to perform specific tasks defined as precisely as possible and in a manner which more and more is patterned after typing pools. The increase in the percentage of coders is likely to be only in the near term, however; as hardware and software innovations make machine-generated code practical, "coders" will give way to machines tended by nonsoftware workers, for example, managers, clerks, or scientific/engineering users.

A second category of software worker is also likely to experience near-term growth and long-term decline. The applications programmer's role will depend on the expanding use of packaged software which requires relatively minor but regular changes to meet customer requirements. Like coders, their future will hinge on the ability of hardware and software developers to simplify the use of hardware. As higher-level languages are created and are combined with improved hardware, the machines will become directly accessible to untrained users. The "man-machine interface" which managers and engineers look forward to is one unmediated by a human programmer.

The obvious implication of the short-run relative increase of coders and applications programmers is that the highly trained specialists who design languages, operating systems, large-scale programming undertakings, and so on, will decrease, at least in the short run, as a proportion of this total software workforce. They will, however, increase in importance; it is their work which defines and gives direction to less skilled workers even as they contribute to the latter's ultimate loss of skill and function.

If the software workforce is transformed, can the training of software workers be far behind? The training of those who do the most routine jobs will be moved—indeed, the move has already started—from universities and engineering schools to junior colleges and even high schools. It seems safe to predict—because it has already happened—that coders and even some applications programmers will receive what is explicitly vocational training as their work is more and more openly bracketed with clerical occupations.

At the other extreme, the training of "creative" workers will continue to be concentrated in the elite science centers—MIT, Cal Tech, and a handful of others—or the science, engineering, or mathematics departments of elite universities. The latter will also train an important part of the technically knowledgeable management and executive pool that oversees the overall direction of electronic data processing.

Finally, the middle range of specialists whose responsibilities are to supervise the immediate application of software and hardware to the practical needs of industry, commerce, and state administration will continue to be trained in conventional engineering schools.

In summary, the training of software workers is likely to reproduce the divisions that already exist in the older, more established engineering occupations. These divisions constitute a stratified system which reflects and helps maintain the hardening divisions between head and hand workers.

We can also expect changes in the kinds of people recruited into the various software suboccupations. The great differences in rewards and in formal training (or at any rate, in formal credentials) will mean sorting out people according to social class background to a much greater degree than now. As long as programming was half magic and half art, talented people capable of doing the work were welcome whatever their credentials. Programming's routinization and its division into creative and routine work, head and hand occupations, high and low paying jobs mean that what made programming different has been eliminated, assuring the occupation an unobtrusive (and indeed obscure) niche in the American workplace. That workplace is stratified not only by race and sex—which recent developments have forced us to acknowledge—but by social class as well, which is harder for Americans to confront. Yet, it is absolutely clear that once a new enterprise or occupation has developed far enough, its open qualities disappear, to be replaced by much more rigid structures of recruitment, training, and advancement. To take by way of example only those occupations closest to programming—both in terms of content and historical development—science and engineering have displayed clear-cut patterns of social divisions. Scientists were recruited from solidly professional and middle class families before the emergence of modern engineering. They remain to this day much more middle class in origin than do the engineering workers, who come from much more modest family backgrounds. Engineers, in turn, are from higher status families on the average than the lowest-ranking scientific workers, the technicians.

Programming itself provides an interesting illustration of how routinization reinforces existing class divisions in the larger society. The edp industries have used equal opportunity laws and affirmative action regulations to replace skilled and expensive workers with cheaper, less skilled workers. As older, white male (and relatively expensive) specialists are phased out of programming, they are being replaced with programmers who are more female and nonwhite as well as less well trained and with fewer formal credentials. They are also paid considerably less on the average.

It should be stressed, to avoid confusing cause and consequence, that the de-skilling of the "average programmer" has not come about *because* of the influx of less skilled women, black and/or brown employees. On the contrary, management-designed routinization has made it possible to use less well trained and less skilled workers to begin with. Women and nonwhites have been brought into the bottom rungs of programming work, as coders and applications programmers, precisely because women and nonwhites have always been the largest sources of cheap labor. Their recent recruitment into software and other edp occupations, nominally in compliance with federal and state requirements, may very well have happened anyway as programming's structure is made to look like the structure of conventional industries.

The future of programmers and programming

It is hard to anticipate a happy future for the majority of software workers, particularly for the newest and least skilled entrants. Not only will their work be further degraded, but recent trends have shown how white collar detail workers are just as vulnerable to layoffs, dismissals, and demands for "increased productivity" as their blue-collar counterparts.

The future well-being and dignity of programmers is further clouded by the faith, so far unshaken, of software workers themselves in the ability and desire of their employers to go on rewarding them for their services. The faith, when combined with a carefully cultivated individualism, produces two major results. The first is an unwillingness to challenge the management's definition of what is going on and how the employee should behave. The second is a commitment to dealing with those problems of work or career which do arise on an individual rather than a collective basis. As a consequence, the individual programmer has no defense, economically or psychologically, when dismissal comes. He or she has no economic defense because there is no one else to back his or her claim to continued employment. There is no psychological defense because the other side of "individual" success is "individual" failure. While step promotions and pay increments were a regular part of employment, such individualism seemed justified. With the "failure" of dismissal, the programmer is thus invited to locate the cause of his/her fall from grace in personal shortcomings. It is a terrible and—if my analysis of the structure of the programming workplace is correct—an unfair burden for the programmer to bear. Unfortunately, programmers are likely to have to go on bearing it for some time yet. The experience of other engineering and technical industries shows that workers in these industries are extremely reluctant to redefine their role in their workplaces or their relations to their employers. Even in times of relative economic crisis in the edp industries—notably 1971–1974— software workers who kept their jobs while friends and colleagues were losing theirs merely felt relieved and did little to resist the unseemly treatment of fellow "professional" workers. Instead, the survivors accepted with little objection management references to "dead wood" and "obsolete" training and shouldered without complaint the added work left by their former colleagues. The routinization of programming is likely to leave such attitudes unaffected.

Reference Braverman, Harry. *Labor and Monopoly Capital: The Degradation of Work in the Twentieth Century* (1974). New York and London: Monthly Review Press.

Appendix

Structured programming For practical purposes, the discussion of structured programming among software workers is limited to high-level technical specialists and managers. Each brings to the discussion a significantly different conception of programming as an activity.

Technical specialists are likely to approach programming as an exercise in mathematics and logic. Programming here is an intellectual undertaking and structured programming has been embraced as a *systematic method of inquiry*. As such it offers orderly thinking, common definitions, standard notation, and so on. Structured programming, in other words, is a way to design, create, and test programs which can be proved in the manner of a mathematical theorem.

Managers, on the other hand, approach programming as a *production process*. Programming is an activity which results in a product (i.e., a program), not in a proof. Furthermore, because it is a production activity which takes place in bureaucratic settings, programming automatically raises the issue of *control*. In short, programming is a social activity which requires management.

Managers have therefore adapted the principles of structured programming—orderliness, simplicity, economical and standard language—to facilitate control over a social process rather than to enhance an intellectual activity.

It is the management, or social control, approach to structured programming which I have emphasized in the present study. For managers, structured programming is attractive because it limits the number and kind of control logic available to the software worker in designing and coding a program.

The allowable control (or ''logic'') structures are, first, a

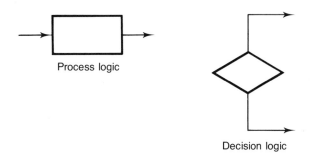

Process logic

Decision logic

FIGURE 1. Basic flowchart elements

"process" instruction or set of instructions. Once indicated, a given process or sequence must be completed before another process or sequence can be initiated.

Naturally, there will be times when it is necessary or desirable to execute a subset of the process or sequence. This requires a different kind of control structure and suggests the second basic control device, the "decision" logic. It is no more than an option to choose between alternative actions, that is, processes or sequences. Figure 1 is a representation of these two basic control logics.

It is necessary in most programs to repeat a process or a decision. In such cases we meet the third control or logic element of structured programming, the repetition or iterative control, which is, however, a combination of the process and decision elements; the decision is either to continue processing or to terminate. See Figure 2.

FIGURE 2. Basic components

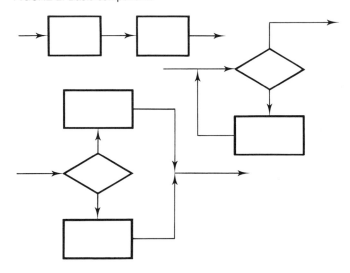

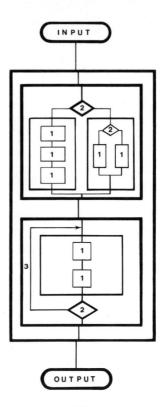

FIGURE 3

With only these three fundamental logic choices, it is possible, in theory, to design and write programs able to control a machine in the performance of the most complex and extensive tasks.

For example, Figure 3 shows several instruction or process sequences (marked 1) and decision processes (marked 2) combined with iterative instructions (marked 3) to form a relatively simple program constructed according to the basic principles of structured program design.

Larger, more complex programs can be built simply by combining similar small-scale programs—which are now labelled ''modules'' or ''subsystems'' or ''subroutines,'' etc.—in a large software exercise.

Index